MW00584418

In the Courts of Three Popes

IN THE COURTS
OF THREE POPES

An American Lawyer and Diplomat

in the Last Absolute Monarchy of the West

MARY ANN GLENDON

IMAGE
New York

Published in the United States by Image, an imprint of Random House,
a division of Penguin Random House LLC, New York.

Image is a registered trademark and the "I" colophon is a trademark
of Penguin Random House LLC.

"Ode for the Eightieth Birthday of Pope John Paul II" from *New and Collected Poems:
1931–2001* by Czeslaw Milosz. Copyright © 1988, 1991, 1995, 2001 by Czeslaw Milosz
Royalties, Inc. Used by permission of HarperCollins Publishers.

John Paul II prayer: © Libreria Editrice Vaticana, used by permission of the *Dicastero per la Communicazione-Libreria Editrice Vaticano*.

"The last meeting with Pope John Paul II." Photography by Servizio Fotografico
Vaticano © Vatican Media, used by permission.

"Welcoming Pope Benedict to the Pontifical Academy." Photography by Servizio
Fotografico Vaticano © Vatican Media, used by permission.

"Emceeing Eunice Kennedy Shriver's eightieth birthday celebration." Photography
by Russ Campbell; copyright © John F. Kennedy Library Foundation, used courtesy of
the John F. Kennedy Library Foundation.

"'Your friend Joe Biden is blocking my confirmation hearing.'" Photography by
Russ Campbell; copyright © John F. Kennedy Library Foundation, used courtesy of
the John F. Kennedy Library Foundation.

"Presentation of credentials to Pope Benedict XVI." Photography by Servizio Fotografico Vaticano © Vatican Media, used by permission.

"The papal welcome at the entrance to the Torre San Giovanni." Photography by
Eric Draper, courtesy of the George W. Bush Presidential Library and Museum.

"With Václav Havel at the 2008 meeting of the Prague Forum 2000." Photography
by Adam Packer, courtesy of Mr. Packer.

"Welcoming the newly elected Pope Francis to the Pontifical Academy." Photography by Servizio Fotografico Vaticano © Vatican Media, used by permission.

"The Institute of Religious Works (the Vatican Bank)." © Pillar Media, used courtesy of Pillar Media.

"Pope Francis opening the IOR board meeting with a prayer." Photography by Servizio Fotografico Vaticano © Vatican Media, used by permission.

Hardcover ISBN 978-0-593-44375-0
Ebook ISBN 978-0-593-44376-7

Printed in the United States of America on acid-free paper

imagecatholicbooks.com

2 4 6 8 9 7 5 3 1

First Edition

In memory of
Martin Francis Glendon
and
Sarah Pomeroy Glendon

Contents

CONTENTS

Introduction

One afternoon in the autumn of 2013, I witnessed an unusual ceremony in the Vatican Library. Two men, Terrence Keeley and Cardinal Raffaele Farina, stood facing each other under a magnificent frescoed ceiling that celebrates the marriage of faith and reason. The American financier's hand rested on a Bible while the cardinal administered a solemn oath, detailing all the unpleasant things that could happen to Terry in this world and the next if he broke his vow. Terry was, in Vatican parlance, being "put under the Pontifical Secret."

Earlier that year, Pope Francis had appointed me, Farina, and three others to a commission that was to investigate the scandal-ridden Vatican Bank, and we had engaged Terry, a managing director of the investment firm BlackRock, as a consultant. Since he would be privy to sensitive information in the course of his work, Farina determined he would need to be sworn to secrecy.

As I watched the time-honored ritual, surrounded by volumes of ancient wisdom, I could not help but reflect that no one had ever thought to put me under pontifical secrecy, even though by that time I had served three pontificates in various capacities for nearly two decades. After a certain point, I suppose, everyone must have assumed that had been done somewhere along the line.

The oversight is revealing of the position of women in a court with many lords and few ladies. In my years of service to the Holy See, I was a stranger in a rather strange land—a layperson in a culture dominated by clergy, an American woman in an environment that was largely male and Italian, and a citizen of a constitutional republic in one of the world's last absolute monarchies.

So different is life in such a court from life in a liberal democracy that I sometimes felt a certain kinship with Mark Twain's Connecticut Yankee who, after a blow to the head, woke up in the Court of King Arthur. My journey also began with romantic, idealistic notions, and I too became a little wiser about courtly life as time passed. Even today, with twenty-four years of service to the Holy See behind me, I remain an outsider looking in.

This book is the story of my experiences with the Holy See and what I saw in the courts of three very different popes as they tried to respond to the challenges and opportunities of a rapidly transforming world.

My work with the Holy See began at a time when the institutional Church was facing multiple crises. These crises and the Church's need to adapt have been especially challenging for laypeople, as I can testify personally.

While talk of the Church's struggles in this relatively new situation often focuses on institutions, bishops, and prelates, it is in fact the laity who bear the primary responsibility for carrying out the Church's mission of evangelization in the secular spheres where they live and work. The Second Vatican Council made clear that it was up to lay men and women, not the clergy, to imbue political, economic, and social institutions with Christian principles.

The council fathers, recognizing that the modern world presented Christianity with formidable new complexities, committed the Church to a process that Pope John XXIII had called *aggiornamento,* literally "updating." But even the most farsighted of those at the council could not have anticipated the social and cultural upheaval that began right when the council was concluding.

The revolution came on so unexpectedly that even professional demographers were caught by surprise. In the span of fifteen years, starting in 1965, birth and marriage rates plummeted in industrialized countries, while rates of divorce and births outside of marriage rose steeply. Every institution, family, and individual was affected in some way by the breakdown in traditional norms, by changing attitudes regarding sex and marriage, and by the mood to "question authority." Increasing numbers of men and women were identifying themselves as nonreligious or nonaffiliated with organized religion.

Pope Saint John Paul II, Pope Benedict XVI, and Pope Francis all had to strive to find better ways to fulfill the Church's mission "at the end of Christendom," as Fulton Sheen described the situation. It was the end, he specified, "not of Christianity, not of the Church, but of Christendom— of economic, social and political life as inspired by Christian principles."

For these three popes, the work of *aggiornamento* meant finding better ways to communicate with modern men and women, reforming inefficient ecclesiastical structures, working to heal old divisions within Christianity, and improving relations with other religions and secular institutions. Those challenges were daunting enough at Vatican II, but they became infinitely more complicated by the end of the twentieth century. And apart from changes in the world, two internal crises were emerging: the scandals of priestly sexual abuse and corruption in the area of Church finances.

It was just at that point—in the mid-1990s—that I became involved in the work of the Holy See.

So while this book is a reflection on what I observed while serving the Holy See, it is also a reflection on the changing role of the laity. This book is the perspective of an American lawyer and laywoman on the dynamics of three papal courts as each pope navigated the enormous cultural changes of the last century. It is my hope that lay Catholics especially will find my account of the ups and downs of that process helpful in their own struggles to be "salt, light, and leaven" during this time of turbulence in the Church and society.

Our own life experiences inform how we understand the present, especially where matters of faith are concerned. And since my religious background inevitably affects my approach to the matters discussed in this memoir, a few words about the most important of my formative influences are in order.

I was raised as a Catholic by Congregationalists in Dalton, a small paper-manufacturing town in the westernmost county of Massachusetts. At the time that my mother, Sarah Pomeroy, a Protestant, married Martin Glendon in the rectory of St. Agnes Church (in those days, "mixed marriages" could not be celebrated in the church itself), the Catholic Church required the non-Catholic spouse to sign a document agreeing that any children of the marriage would be raised as Catholics. For my mother, that was a serious obligation, not because it was a contract but because it was a promise.

In the large Pomeroy clan, where my brother, Martin; my sister, Julia; and I were raised, it was not only my mother who took the promise seriously. Grandmother Pomeroy gave me a rosary for my First Communion (along with a little book called *One God,* with a Christian, a Jew, and a Muslim on the cover). When I stayed with aunts and uncles during summer holidays, they made sure I went to Sunday Mass, driving me to the church and waiting outside in their car until the service was over. Grandfather Pomeroy was not much of a church-goer. He was, as his minister said in the funeral eulogy, a man who believed in "simple virtues, the democratic process, and the future of America." The minister made special mention of Theodore Pomeroy's ecumenism long before the word came into vogue:

> He respected the faiths of other men, and he had a per-sonal and deep faith of his own. "I've seen them all," he used to say. "They all have good men and work for the same things." Several years ago when a Roman Catholic priest spoke in our church for the first time, he was at the head of the line to shake his hand and say that he thought it was a "wonderful thing" to happen to both our faiths.

The Pomeroys were not the only people in my family with an appreciation of religious and ethnic differences that went beyond tolerance. My father's brother Mickey and his Protes-tant wife, Margaret, had three children, one of whom, my cousin Lowell, became a Sulpician priest, and another, my cousin Barbara, an Ursuline sister. During all the years before Barbara traded in her traditional religious attire for polyester pantsuits, Aunt Margaret made Barbara's habits on her old Singer sewing machine. Without doubt, the kindness and goodwill of our Protestant relatives played an enormous role in the religious commitments my cousins and I made later on. The spirit that guided those wonderful old Yankees was a marvelous blend of their religious beliefs and the ethos of neighborly accommodation that pervaded the almost-lost world of small New England townships.

My father was quite content to leave the religious education of his children in the hands of the Pomeroys and the nuns who came from Pittsfield once a week to teach Sunday School at St. Agnes parish. Thanks to those Sisters of St. Joseph and the *Baltimore Catechism* (the standard Catholic teaching text in the United States until the 1960s), I acquired a rudimentary but sound foundation in Catholic doctrine. One of the more consequential Catholic sensibilities I acquired at this time came from an article I read in high school. I was just becoming dimly aware that proponents of psychological, economic, and biological theories tend to treat their theories as total philosophies, and I came across a newspaper column by Father Theodore Hesburgh, the president of the University of Notre Dame. He wrote that "when you encounter a conflict between science and religion, you're either dealing with a bad scientist or a bad theologian." The sentence jumped out at me, and it is no exaggeration to say that it had a powerful influence on my intellectual development. Years later, when I got to know Father Ted, it was a joy to be able to thank him for that gift. His advice not only helped me on the perilous journey from childhood beliefs to adult faith but also served to channel some of my adolescent energy toward a robust but critical engagement with the natural and human sciences.

In the 1940s, there were still many similarities between Dalton and the self-governing New England townships that

Alexis de Tocqueville visited in 1831, and which he celebrated in *Democracy in America*. Nestled along the Housatonic River in the Berkshire Hills, with some five thousand inhabitants, Dalton was the size that Aristotle envisioned for an ideal city. There was still a town meeting, where citizens decided many important matters, and a Board of Selectmen, of which my father was the first Irish Catholic Democrat to be elected chairman. My grandfather Pomeroy was chairman of the town Republican committee.

By the 1940s, Catholics of Irish, Italian, and Polish descent accounted for about half of Dalton's inhabitants. There was a small African American community, whose ancestors had come north on the Underground Railroad and established a thriving tree surgeon business, and one Jewish family—that of the high school English teacher who taught me to love poetry. He later became the principal and then the superintendent of schools. The town doctor, a gruff old Scot who liked to recite Tennyson to his patients, made a point of letting everyone know he was an atheist.

The two churches with the largest congregations were on opposite sides of Main Street. A stranger driving through Dalton might well have taken St. Agnes's Catholic Church for a Protestant meetinghouse. From the outside, it was a white wooden building like many seen on New England village greens. But inside, its stained-glass windows, the Latin liturgy, the Stations of the Cross, and the statues of Mary, Joseph, and Saint Agnes told that it had been built by a different kind of immigrant from the early settlers.

For me, my mother's solid gray granite Congregational meetinghouse and my father's church with its heavenward spire marked out the contours of a spiritual universe where much was held in common. Life had been hard for almost everyone during the recent Depression, members of both communities "took in" people who could not fend for themselves, women knitted socks for our soldiers during World War II, and schoolkids assembled "CARE packages" for suffering Europeans when the conflict ended. Every school day began with saluting the flag and reciting the Lord's Prayer, with the Catholic kids falling silent after "Deliver us from evil" and the Protestants carrying on sturdily with the "For Thine is the kingdom" part until the Catholics came in again for the final "Amen."

By being immersed in both the social-justice-focused Congregationalist community and the pious Catholic community, I learned to hold both commitments, to the common good and to the life of faith, as one. By the 1950s, Congregationalism in Dalton bore few traces of its stern Puritan origins. Unlike the Catholics, who took the obligation to attend Mass very seriously, most of the town's Protestants had a more relaxed attitude toward Sunday services. My mother's church was, however, a beehive of charitable and social activities. The women organized a never-ending round of events and benefits that the whole town, Protestants and Catholics alike, thoroughly enjoyed: bake sales, potluck suppers, white elephant sales, talent shows, clambakes, and so on. During Lent, Congregational families saved spare change in colorful little calico sacks, which were brought to church on Easter Sunday for distribution to worthy charities. When my sister, Julia, and I traveled to the March on Washington in the summer of 1963, it was on a bus chartered by a group of Berkshire County Protestants determined to do their part in delivering on what Martin Luther King Jr., in his "I Have a Dream" speech, would call the promissory note of equality. Some were following in the steps of their ancestors who had fought in the Civil War.

The groups and events at St. Agnes had a very different focus. There were no suppers, no sales, no shows, but many novenas, recitations of the rosary, benedictions, and adorations of the Blessed Sacrament. After every Mass, we prayed for the conversion of Russia. During Lent, we fasted, confessed our sins, did penance, and promised to amend our lives. Exactly contrary to the oft-asserted theological distinction, Dalton's Protestants were virtuosos of good works while the Catholics were virtuosos of faith. Immersed in both cultures, I was destined to be a student of comparative law and government.

Rome and its popes barely figured in the routines of Catholic life in Dalton. When our parish priest Father Leo Shaughnessy announced one Sunday in 1957 that Pius XII had relaxed the rule on abstention from food and water from midnight until after receiving communion the next morning, it caused quite a stir. People gathered outside after Mass to discuss this remarkable innovation. For many, it was a relief to be told that we could now at least have a glass of water in that period. But others were uneasy about departing from the requirement of strict abstinence before receiving the Holy Eucharist. "Those Italians," said one man, "can drink all the water they want, but I'm not doing it."

It was not that we lacked the sense of belonging to a universal Church. For me, Catholicism before Vatican II was a window opening out to the world beyond the Berkshires. Its ceremonies spoke of a history before Plymouth Rock, and its liturgy linked us to every Catholic on earth. Through the words and gestures of the Latin Mass, we were connected to villagers in places where it never snowed, to inhabitants of great cities like Rome and New York, and to our own ancestors buried in faraway lands. The Church enabled the sons and daughters of mill workers to understand themselves as members of the rich tapestry of world history, and in the unfolding mystery of salvation.

Thanks to the *Baltimore Catechism,* we also learned that, unlike our Protestant friends and neighbors (and my maternal relatives), we were part of one Church headed by one man who was the successor of Peter and therefore the Vicar of Christ on earth. And for as long as anyone could remember, that man was an Italian.

To grow up in Dalton in the forties and fifties was to be immersed in local patriotism, biblical faith, a sense of a future filled with opportunities, and, yes, in my case rather romanticized ideas about faraway Rome. Never did I imagine, however, that I would one day travel there as a consultant to the Holy See.

PART I

The Court of John Paul II

Then, suddenly, like the clear sound of the bell for matins,
Your sign of dissent, which is like a miracle.
People ask, not comprehending, how it's possible
That the young of the unbelieving countries
Gather in the public square, shoulder to shoulder,
Waiting for news from two thousand years ago
And throw themselves at the feet of the Vicar
Who embraced with his love the whole human tribe.

You are with us and will be with us henceforth.
When the forces of chaos raise their voice
And the owners of truth lock themselves in churches
And only the doubters remain faithful,
Your portrait in our homes every day reminds us
How much one man can accomplish and how sainthood works.

—FROM CZESLAW MILOSZ,
"Ode for the Eightieth Birthday of Pope John Paul II"

CHAPTER ONE

From Dalton to Rome

✤

*I thought I knew everything when I came to Rome, but I
soon found I had everything to learn.*

—EDMONIA LEWIS, American sculptor

I attended the University of Chicago at a time when the wags
used to say that it was the university where Jewish professors
taught Thomas Aquinas to Marxist students. Works by Augustine and Aquinas were taught by the likes of Richard
Weaver, Leo Strauss, and Richard McKeon. Catholic lumi-
naries like Jacques Maritain and Martin D'Arcy were frequently on campus for long visits. I became acquainted with
the riches of the Catholic intellectual tradition through the
core "great books" curriculum installed by Robert Maynard
Hutchins, who once referred to the Catholic Church somewhat enviously as having "the longest intellectual tradition of
any institution in the world," and who drew freely from that
tradition in constructing Chicago's mandatory core of courses.
Not only did I thus become familiar with the "greats" in my
own tradition but I observed that those thinkers were held in
high esteem by the best Chicago teachers.

The same education that reinforced a critical approach to
learning also helped reinforce the religious habits and practices I had acquired in Dalton. Especially significant to my
formation was the work of Thomas Aquinas. He understood

the intellect as a gift from God—a gift whose use would advance one's ability to better know, love, and serve the Creator. I absorbed a little of Thomas's approach to knowledge, which had enabled him to engage pagan philosophy with confidence that his desire to know would not unsettle his faith but rather bring him closer to the mind of God.

As in the case of many Catholics of my generation, my education gave me a lively appreciation for the spiritual and intellectual riches of Catholicism, but I had minimal exposure to Catholic social thought, the body of Church teaching about economic and political matters. That changed with the appearance of Pope John XXIII's famous encyclical *Pacem in Terris,* "Peace on Earth."

It was the spring of 1963, and I was in Belgium, finishing a year of graduate legal studies at the fiercely secular Université Libre de Bruxelles and working as an intern at the headquarters of the European Common Market, the predecessor of the European Union. I had been active in social causes as an undergraduate and a law student at the University of Chicago, and so I was excited that the pope himself was endorsing the ideals I believed in. His emphatic insistence that "racial discrimination can in no way be accepted," his affirmation of women's roles and rights in contemporary society, and his praise for the Universal Declaration of Human Rights gave me a feeling of pride that my Church was in the vanguard of historic changes.

For an American Catholic like me, it was also a certain source of pride to see the wide public attention that the encyclical commanded. For the first time in history, a papal encyclical—a letter traditionally circulated to churches—made use of modern human rights language. Moreover, it was addressed to "all men of good will," which attracted notice beyond religious circles. *The New York Times* published it in full, and over two thousand prominent statespersons, scholars, and diplomats from all parts of the world attended a United Nations conference devoted to the document.

The UN's Universal Declaration of Human Rights—which was being debated in Paris while Angelo Roncalli, who later became Pope John XXIII, was papal nuncio to France—became an important point of reference for the Church when speaking to a secular society. Because the declaration had come to serve as a model for most post–World War II rights declarations and was instrumental for cross-national discussions of human freedom and dignity, it made good sense for the pope to invoke it. In later years, both John Paul II and Benedict XVI would follow John XXIII's example, drawing upon the declaration while also expressing reservations about its susceptibility to misuse.

Although *Pacem in Terris* captivated me, and though I was excited by the Second Vatican Council, I fell out of touch with much of what was happening in the Church for a few years in the 1960s when I drifted toward what today would be called cafeteria Catholicism.

A painful personal crisis, however, brought me up short. In May 1966, my beloved father died at age fifty-five of a rapidly advancing cancer that had been diagnosed only three months earlier. Ten days after Dad's death, my daughter Elizabeth was born, and shortly after that Elizabeth's father—an African American lawyer I had met in the civil rights movement—moved on to other interests. I found myself with sole responsibility for a beautiful little baby girl, far from friends and relatives, and I was forced to face the fact that my own decisions—a civil marriage to a person I barely knew—had brought me to this pass.

I decided that I would leave my job as an associate in the Chicago law firm of Mayer, Brown & Platt and move back to Massachusetts so that I would be closer to my mother, who was then suffering from mental problems, and to my teenage brother and sister, who were devastated by the unexpected loss of our father.

Unsure about how best to transition back to Massachusetts, I consulted one of my mentors at the University of Chicago Law School, Soia Mentschikoff, who had been the first woman to teach law at Harvard. Soia put me in touch with the Dean of Boston College Law School, Father Robert Drinan, who invited me for an interview that led quickly to a job offer.

In the summer of 1968, I moved back to Massachusetts with Elizabeth to begin my academic career. The Boston College environment was a great help to my spiritual life. I was surrounded by faithful Catholic colleagues who became good friends, and I was welcomed to participate in interdisciplinary projects by the learned Jesuit who chaired the philosophy department, Joseph Flanagan. Through regular prayer, Mass attendance, and the imperative to be the best mother I could be, I became a better Catholic. And through Boston College study groups, I received something like a graduate education in theology while reading and discussing works by Romano Guardini, Karl Rahner, Joseph Ratzinger, Bernard Lonergan, and others. These interdisciplinary sessions helped me to see legal problems in relation to the manifold challenges that the Church was facing in a secularizing postmodern world.

Two years later, it was my great blessing to be married in a Catholic ceremony to Edward Lev, with whom I had worked at Mayer, Brown & Platt, and who moved his labor law practice to Boston. It was a time of incredible blessing. Edward adopted Elizabeth, our daughter Katherine was born, Edward won the American Bar Association's Ross Essay prize for a brilliant article on arbitration, and I was well on the way to tenure with the publication of a text with Max Rheinstein, who had been my supervisor in the University of Chicago's Master of Comparative Law program. In 1973, in gratitude "to Whom it may concern" (as my Jewish husband would say), we adopted an adorable three-year-old Korean orphan, whom we named Sarah Pomeroy Lev after my mother, who had died earlier that year.

Throughout the 1970s, family life and work as a beginning law professor occupied nearly all of my time and attention. For better or worse, most of that eventful decade—the Vietnam debacle, the pontificate of Paul VI, the immediate aftermath of Vatican II, Watergate, Woodstock, *Roe v. Wade,* the Iran hostage crisis—just passed me by. My one effort to serve the Church in that period was a disaster. Teaching law students was a breeze compared to a catechism class for eighth graders!

In October 1978, when Karol Wojtyla stood on a balcony overlooking the Piazza San Pietro and introduced himself as "a Pope from a faraway land," I had no idea how that event would change the world and affect the rest of my life. The following year, when the new pope, John Paul II, visited Boston, the only member of our family who went (in pouring rain) to hear him speak was Elizabeth, then twelve years old.

When I was ready to devote time to pro bono activities, I

scarcely recognized the causes to which I had once been devoted. I remained intensely interested in care for our natural environment, in human rights, and in issues affecting women and families and the world of work. But I couldn't see how to engage with the movements that were then dominant in those areas. My dissatisfaction with these trends eventually led me to look for better approaches in organizations grounded in Catholic social thought. In the Berkshires of my youth, I had been steeped in what we called conservationism. Berkshire natives were already concerned about the dangerous chemicals that Pittsfield's General Electric plant was dumping into the Housatonic River and vigilant about the need to protect Mount Greylock from commercial exploitation. My grandfather Pomeroy enrolled me in the National Wildlife Federation when I was ten. So I was drawn to the new field of environmental law. But the mood and tone of the environmental movement in the seventies was so focused on population control as to seem almost anti-people. It seemed distant from the concept of stewardship for all of God's creation.

The political landscape had changed too. As a college student, I had been proud to cast my first vote in a presidential election for Massachusetts's own John F. Kennedy, and as a law student and young lawyer, I had been active in the great cause of the day—the struggle to end segregation. But both the Democratic Party and the civil rights movement had become unwelcoming to those of us who believed that Martin Luther King's "Beloved Community" required concern for unborn life and assistance for mothers who needed support. At the same time, the Republican Party was not very welcoming to persons who admired many aspects of FDR's New Deal. So I became and have remained an Independent.

There was also the particular form of feminism that became dominant in the 1970s. When students have asked me whether I am a feminist, I have always replied, "Yes, if that means I have an interest in issues that are of concern mainly or mostly to women." My concept of feminism had been shaped by Berkshire County's own Susan B. Anthony, who fought for women's suffrage and believed that abortion chiefly benefited irresponsible men. It was hard for me to relate to a movement that harbored animosity to men, marriage, and motherhood, and that emphasized abortion rights.

And so, as my children grew older, I devoted most of my pro bono activities to Catholic organizations. I became active in Church affairs both in the Boston Archdiocese and at the national level as a consultant to the U.S. Bishops Conference Committee on International Policy (now the Committee on International Justice and Peace). The Archbishop of Boston, Bernard Law, and I had much in common. We had both been raised by a Catholic father and a Protestant mother, and we had both been engaged in the struggle for civil rights in Mississippi, he as the crusading editor of a local Catholic newspaper and I as a volunteer attorney for civil rights workers who had been arrested. One of his first innovations in Boston was to establish an advisory committee on social justice, which I eagerly joined.

The members of this new committee were a diverse group of business and labor leaders, academics, and health care professionals. Its chair, Monsignor William Murphy, who had just come from Rome after serving for several years at the Pontifical Council for Justice and Peace, understood well that our advice was not going to be useful if our understanding of social justice came out of the secular mindset that prevailed in the places where most of us worked. So he made it a priority to provide us with a few tutorials. He sent us each a copy of Pope John Paul II's encyclical *Sollicitudo Rei Socialis,* "On Social Concern," which had just appeared, and he arranged for one of the pope's closest associates, Belgian Cardinal Jan Schotte, to speak at our first meeting. Cardinal Schotte, who had served with Murphy on the Justice and Peace Council, spoke to us about the principles that we would be expected to bring to bear on social justice issues in the archdiocese. He called our attention to a passage on the role of the laity:

> It is appropriate to emphasize the *preeminent role* that belongs to the *laity,* both men and women. . . . It is their task to animate temporal realities with Christian commitment, by which they show that they are witnesses and agents of peace and justice. [emphasis in original]

Most of us needed that wake-up call. Monsignor Murphy was determined to pound into our heads that it was primarily up to us laypeople, and not the clergy, to bring the principles of Catholic social teaching to life in the secular spheres where we live and work. Happily, my work on these committees meshed well with my academic work. The topics I had chosen for comparative study—the family, the world of work, church-state issues—were central to the Church's teachings on social and economic questions. Most of my research and writing was focused on how the legal systems of countries at comparable stages of development handled problems with which the United States was currently struggling, especially in the world of work and family life. In my book *The New Family and the New Property,* I traced the shift that was occur-

ring in the relative importance of family, labor force participation, and government as determinants of wealth, social
standing, sense of worth, and economic security.

It was just after its publication, and while I was doing further research on labor and employment law, that I encountered the thought of Pope John Paul II in his 1981 encyclical
Laborem Exercens, "On Human Work," the most personal of
his encyclicals, and also his favorite. According to papal biographer George Weigel, it was based in part on Wojtyla's own
experiences as a manual laborer during the German occupa-
tion of Poland.

The encyclical put on display the pope's empathy for the
everyday struggles of men and women, his deep faith, and his
sense of history. I was struck by the fact that he addressed
himself to "the sons and daughters of the Church" and "all
men and women of good will." The pope's linkage of work
and family, his emphasis on human rights, and his global approach were so congenial to me that I was moved to read further in Catholic writings on social and political issues.

Around the same time, my husband made an observation
that was to have a long-lasting effect on my professional life.
One autumn when I returned to Boston College Law School
after the summer recess, I noticed that someone had taken
down all the crucifixes from the classroom walls. Together
with the other Catholic professors, I wondered who had done
that and why, but we soon dropped the subject and went on
to something else. That evening, when I told Edward about
it, he was astonished. "Why do you Catholics put up with that
kind of thing?" he asked. "There would be an uproar if anyone did something like that at Brandeis."

That was a transformational moment for me. I asked myself: Why *do* we Catholics put up with that sort of thing? Why *do* we get so careless about the faith for which our ancestors made so many sacrifices? I recalled something that priest-sociologist Andrew Greeley once told me. Of all the minority groups in this country, he said, Catholics were the least concerned about their own rights and the least conscious of the persistent and systematic discrimination against them and our faith.

For a long time in the United States, Catholic immigrants were subjected to discrimination and prejudice. When my father graduated from college and looked for a job as a teacher in the public schools, he was told plainly by many employers that they didn't hire Irish or Catholics. Under such conditions, many Catholics adopted one of two survival strategies, what I call the "way of the turtle" and the "way of the chameleon." The turtles kept their spiritual lives private, inside their shells, in a separate compartment from the rest of their lives. The chameleons changed their color enough to blend in with their surroundings, and if some part of their Catholic heritage didn't fit in, they just set it aside.

As a pro-life feminist, I was safe from becoming a turtle or a chameleon, but up until the crucifix incident, I tended to ignore or shrug off manifestations of anti-Catholic bias. With Edward's question, however, I saw the situation anew. I joined the Catholic League for Religious and Civil Rights, and later on, when my family responsibilities lightened, I devoted a good deal of my time to the cause of religious freedom, national and international. The crucifixes were never restored to the classrooms at Boston College Law School, nor is the word *Catholic* to be found on its website.

By the 1980s, my books and articles had begun to gain a certain recognition, and I was receiving offers for visiting professorships and invitations to give lectures in the United States and abroad. I declined most of them due to family obligations. But I accepted a visit to nearby Harvard in 1974, and I could not resist an invitation to be a visiting professor at my alma mater, the University of Chicago. In the fall of 1984, while teaching at Chicago, I gave the Rosenthal Lectures at Northwestern University, a series of three talks on changing legal approaches to abortion and divorce in twenty-three countries.

Shortly thereafter, I received a call from Harvard Law School Dean James Vorenberg, who wanted to discuss the possibility of my joining the Harvard faculty, and then invited me to give a "job talk" at the law school. When I asked the dean whether he had any suggestions about topics, he said whatever I was currently working on would be fine. I replied that I would be glad to give a report on the findings of my comparative study of abortion law, after which there was a long pause on the other end of the line.

On the appointed day, I presented the results of my study, which showed that U.S. abortion law after *Roe v. Wade,* and its companion case *Doe v. Bolton,* was more permissive than that of other Western nations. Heeding Clifford Geertz's advice that a country's law "is part of a distinctive manner of imagining the real," I made an effort to discern what images of personhood, rights and responsibilities, and human flourishing were being conveyed by each country's approach to abortion, divorce, and economic dependency. I tried to determine what stories were being told, what symbols were being deployed, and what visions were being projected by each country's approach to a range of knotty legal problems—and to shed light on what was distinctive about the way our own legal system was treating those issues.

A few days after my talk, Albert Sacks, a constitutional law professor who had previously been dean, took me out for lunch and said in a friendly way, "You know, no one who was in that room agrees with you on the abortion issue." I reminded him of how severely he and several other respected constitutionalists had criticized *Roe* when it was first decided, mainly on the ground that there was no constitutional warrant for such an intrusion by the Supreme Court into the legislative realm. I asked him why he and so many others had changed their minds. "Well," he said in a burst of candor, "I suppose it was because we came to realize it was very important to the women in our lives."

When Jim Vorenberg called to tell me that the vote in favor of my appointment was "as close to unanimous as it gets these days," I readily accepted. I was sad to leave my friends and colleagues at Boston College, but I was greatly looking forward to having access to Harvard's remarkable foreign law collection and to working with Harvard's distinguished comparatist John P. Dawson, an old New Dealer with whom I had much in common.

In January 1986, just before taking up my new duties at Harvard, I made a weeklong silent retreat at Eastern Point, the Jesuit retreat center situated on a lonely stretch of rocky coast in Gloucester, Massachusetts. Those cold, dark days of prayer and meditation, punctuated by walks in the freezing wind, convinced me of two things: I was not cut out for the contemplative life, and I needed to prepare myself for an academic environment where there would be few people who shared my interests and personal commitments.

My first faculty meeting at Harvard Law School was like nothing I had ever witnessed at Boston College, where civility was taken for granted despite profound disagreements on pedagogical, political, and social issues. Within minutes after the meeting started, one of my new Harvard colleagues used the f-word and another called the dean a liar.

At Boston College, I had a view from my office window of the crucifix above the chapel, which had helped to keep everything in perspective. My Harvard office also had a view of a church, this one topped by a weather vane. But to paraphrase Bob Dylan, I didn't need a weather vane to know which way the wind was blowing. Happily, one of my students provided me with just the right thing. Paolo Carozza, now a friend, coauthor, fellow comparatist, and professor of law and political science at Notre Dame, gave me a copy of Thomas Aquinas's "Prayer Before Studying." I have kept it in my center desk drawer ever since:

Creator of all things,
true Source of light and wisdom,
lofty origin of all being,
graciously let a ray of Your brilliance
penetrate into the darkness of my understanding
and take from me the double darkness
in which I have been born,
an obscurity of both sin and ignorance.
Give me a sharp sense of understanding,
a retentive memory,
and the ability to grasp things correctly and fundamentally.

Grant me the talent of being exact in my explanations,
and the ability to express myself with thoroughness and
    charm.
Point out the beginning,
direct the progress,
and help in completion;
through Christ our Lord. Amen.

I also benefited from a great kindness on the part of Al
Sacks. In anticipation of the bicentennial of the U.S. Constitution, Dean Vorenberg had asked Al to come up with ideas
for marking the occasion at the law school. Al proposed holding an international conference and, aiming to integrate me
into the Harvard environment, suggested that I should chair
the organizing committee. That mitzvah at the very outset of
my Harvard career paid great dividends for me over the
years.

As chair of the bicentennial committee, I had an ample
budget to assemble a remarkable array of speakers—
constitutional experts, political theorists, and activists from
all parts of the world. I was acquainted with many of the
leading European jurists of the day, and, having accompanied Max Rheinstein to several academic events at European
universities, I had developed a few ideas about how to improve on the usual American legal conference. The result was
a gathering of academic stars and democracy activists from
Europe, Africa, the USSR, and Asia, culminating in a gala
dinner at Harvard's Fogg Museum.

The opportunity to arrange such a conference down to the
last detail prepared me well for the events I would have to
organize later as president of the UNESCO-sponsored Inter-

national Association of Legal Science, President of the Pontifical Academy of Social Sciences, and U.S. Ambassador to the Holy See. It also taught me to try to follow the generous example of Al Sacks and to "pay it forward" with opportunities for young men and women seeking to enter environments that might be inhospitable to them or their beliefs.

It was also during my first year on the Harvard faculty that I met Diarmuid Martin, a young Irish monsignor serving in the Vatican as Under Secretary of the Pontifical Council for Justice and Peace. The future Archbishop of Dublin was on a tour sponsored by the U.S. Information Agency, and I was on his list of people to see. He was an entertaining conversationalist, very smart, fluent in Italian, French, and German, with a keen sense of humor—all qualities that I came to appreciate even more when we worked together on the Holy See's delegation to the UN's Beijing Conference on Women in 1995.

It's likely that Diarmuid's visit to me was on the recommendation of his friend and former colleague from the pontifical council, Monsignor William Murphy, with whom I was working on Boston's archdiocesan social justice committee. And although I cannot be certain what led to my recruitment a few years later into the administration of Pope John Paul II, it's likely that Monsignor (now Bishop) Murphy had something to do with it.

One of the first tasks he assigned me on our local committee was to prepare comments on the draft text of a pastoral letter on women being prepared by the U.S. Conference of Catholic Bishops. And apparently my memo was appreciated, because when the pope himself issued an Apostolic Letter to Women, *Mulieris Dignitatem,* in August 1988,

Monsignor Murphy asked me for some reflections on that text as well.

I was expecting the letter to women to be a dry ecclesiastical document. Instead, what struck me most upon reading *Mulieris Dignitatem* was the pope's sympathetic attention to issues that were important to me, both as a scholar and as the mother of three daughters. While tracking developments in family law, I was concerned that even as women acquired more rights than ever before, the role of motherhood was becoming less valued and more difficult, especially for women raising children alone. It was heartening to see that the pope understood that concern. Affirming women's dignity and equality in the strongest possible terms, he pointed out that the ideology of individualism is misplaced where dependents such as children, the sick, and the frail elderly are concerned, and where those who care for them (mostly women) often become dependent themselves in so doing.

What made John Paul II's writing so refreshing was that he drew on his own experiences. When Karol Wojtyla was a young priest, he hiked, skied, and kayaked with male and female friends, including many married couples, coming to know their joys, sorrows, and deepest concerns. Those friendships, and that ease with women and laypeople, continued throughout his life. No pope in living memory ever had so many friendships with lay women and men, as pastor, companion, and confidant.

He began *Mulieris Dignitatem* by quoting these stirring words from the Closing Message of the Second Vatican Council: "The hour is coming, in fact has come, when the vocation of women is being acknowledged in its fullness, the hour in which women acquire in the world an influence, an effect and a power never hitherto achieved." He recalled how many of Christ's most important teachings had first been given to women and reminded the reader of how extraordinary Christ's attitude toward women had been in the context of his time. He recounted how even the disciples were amazed when they went looking for Jesus one day and found him in deep conversation with a Samaritan woman at the well of Jacob. They "marveled that he was talking with a woman" (John 4:27).

The same pastoral approach that would later pervade *Evangelium Vitae,* "The Gospel of Life," was already on display in *Mulieris Dignitatem.* Citing the biblical account of the woman about to be punished for adultery while the sins of her male accusers went unnoticed, the pope wrote:

> How often, in a similar way, *the woman pays* for her own sin (maybe it is she, in some cases, who is guilty of the "other's sin"—the sin of the man), but she alone pays and she pays *all alone*! How often is she abandoned with her pregnancy, when the man, the child's father, is unwilling to accept responsibility for it? [emphasis in original]

I was also impressed by the letter's modesty. John Paul II chose to put his thoughts about the dignity of women in the form of a meditation, an invitation for the reader to join him in reflection about what it means to be a woman or a man. There may still be much to learn, he suggested, about "the anthropological and theological bases that are needed in order to solve the problems connected with the meaning and dignity of being a woman and being a man."

It seemed to me, I wrote to Monsignor Murphy, that the pope was hoping by this letter to inspire women themselves to come up with better ways of thinking and talking about the roles of women in contemporary societies.

Shortly after I sent him my comments, Monsignor Murphy called to tell me that *L'Osservatore Romano* wanted to publish them. That article, I am sure, was responsible for many invitations I later received from the Holy See.

The following year, 1989, saw the publication of my book *The Transformation of Family Law,* in which I noted how the role of motherhood was becoming risky due to what I called the "four deadly Ds": increased chance of divorce, disrespect for nonmarket work, disadvantage in the workplace for women who take time out for family responsibilities, and the destitution that afflicts so many female-headed families.

A few years later, I was excited to learn that I had been selected by Pope John Paul II to be one of the initial members of his newly founded Pontifical Academy of Social Sciences, a body he formed "to aid the Church in the study and development of her social doctrine." This was a perfect fit with all of my academic interests, and it sounded like a great opportunity to support the process of keeping Catholic social teachings up to date.

Then, in the summer of 1995, I received a more challenging assignment. Cardinal Law called to say, "The Holy Father wants you to lead the Holy See delegation to the UN's Fourth World Conference on Women in Beijing this fall."

CHAPTER TWO

Leading a Vatican Delegation: Beijing 1995

✣

I appeal to all men in the Church to undergo, where necessary, a change of heart and to implement as a demand of their faith, a positive vision of women. I ask them to become more and more aware of the disadvantages to which women, and especially girls, have been exposed and to see where the attitude of men, their lack of sensitivity or lack of responsibility, may be at the root.

—JOHN PAUL II, Letter to Mary Ann Glendon
and the Holy See's Delegation to the Fourth World Conference
on Women

As the universal human rights idea began to show its power in the events that led to the demise of Eastern European communism, numerous special interest groups became active in international settings, hoping to have their agenda items recognized as international human rights. Among the best funded and most determined were advocates of aggressive population control and other supporters of abortion rights. At the 1984 Mexico City Conference on Population and Development, both the United States under the Reagan administration and the Holy See had been instrumental in rebuffing efforts to have abortion declared a human right. But the United States and the Holy See found themselves at odds ten years later at the Cairo Conference on Population and Development, where the Clinton administration led an unsuccessful campaign to have abortion rights inserted into what became the steering document for the UN's Population Fund. In the summer of 1995, when I was asked to head the Holy See delegation to the UN's Fourth World Conference on Women in Beijing, it seemed inevitable that the battle would be renewed.

I was daunted by the prospect of leading the Holy See's delegation into that fray, but I felt well equipped by virtue of my cross-national research on the social and legal status of women and my experience as president of the UNESCO-affiliated International Association of Legal Science. My only hesitation was due to the fact that I was hardly a model Catholic, since I had been married and divorced under the civil law before my Catholic marriage to Edward Lev. I explained my concern to Joaquín Navarro-Valls, who, as head of the Holy See Press Office, would be accompanying the Holy See delegation to Beijing. The Spanish psychiatrist turned journalist was a close friend of the pope, and I had great confidence in his judgment. A few days later, Navarro emailed me that he had discussed the matter with "the Boss," who had said it was not a problem. As things turned out, the difficult years that I had spent as the single mother of a biracial child gave me a perspective on women's issues that many of the other participants in the conference lacked.

I also consulted Navarro on protocol. I knew there would be a formal and televised meeting with Pope John Paul II in Rome before the delegation proceeded to China, and I was wondering whether I should bow and kiss the pope's ring on that occasion. "No," said Navarro, "he wants you to look him straight in the eye and shake his hand."

I soon learned that the pope's attitude toward such matters was not shared by all of his brother bishops. A few months later, when I was introduced to the elderly French Cardinal Paul Poupard and I extended my hand, he looked as though he had bitten into a bad escargot. At that moment I resolved to be on the safe side the next time I met a prelate. That happened to be an Irish bishop who, when I said, "Your Excellency" and started to bow, pulled me up by the shoulders, kissed my hand, and said, "Your Beautifulship." (*Welcome to the universal Church,* I thought.)

As I worked on my opening statement for Beijing, I relied on a remarkable series of essays and talks in which Pope John Paul II meditated on women's roles, repeatedly emphasizing that the Christian faith gives no room for oppression based on sex. To the surprise of many, he adopted much of the language of modern feminism, calling women's liberation a "great journey" that "must go on." After meeting with the pope that June, the Secretary General of the Beijing Conference, Gertrude Mongella, told reporters, "If everyone thought as he does, perhaps we wouldn't need a women's conference."

On August 29, the pope met with me and several members of the Holy See delegation just before our departure for China. I expected that either he or someone from the Secretariat of State would give us some specific guidance or instructions. But that did not happen.

The pope read a short message expressing his wish for the success of the conference "in its aim to guarantee all the women of the world 'equality, development, and peace' through full respect for their equal dignity and for their inalienable human rights, so that they can make their full contribution to the good of society."[1] He committed the Holy See to giving special attention to the care and education of girls and young women, especially the most disadvantaged, over the coming years. Then he added some forceful words addressed to "all men in the Church":

> I appeal to all men in the Church to undergo, where necessary, a change of heart and *to implement as a demand of their faith, a positive vision of women*. I ask them to become more and more aware of the disadvantages to which women, and especially girls, have been exposed and to see where the attitude of men, their lack of sensitivity or lack of responsibility, may be at the root. [emphasis added]

In a few private words with me, the Holy Father said that I was "going over there to be a voice for the voiceless." He advised me to rely on the Holy Spirit, and he added a practical suggestion: if I ran into difficulties in the conference, I should consider going over their heads to the press.

The Holy See delegation was by far the most diverse delegation at the Beijing conference, a group of fourteen women and eight men from nine countries and five continents. It was obvious that the composition of the delegation, as well as the decision to appoint a woman as its head, arose from the desire to counter the caricature of the Vatican representatives at a UN conference in Cairo the year before as anti-woman, anti-sex, and in favor of unrestrained procreation.

Among the Beijing delegates was Diarmuid Martin, a skilled negotiator, a veteran of the Cairo conference, and a young man clearly on the rise in the Holy See. Another clerical delegate, Archbishop Renato Martino, was a portly, pink-cheeked man with the practiced cordiality of one who is always "on." He was a longtime Vatican diplomat and had headed the Holy See delegation to the conference in Cairo. He greeted me heartily when we were introduced by the pope, but I was a little concerned when he remarked to me later that "some of my friends say it's not right that a woman should be the boss of an archbishop." I made a point of asking his advice, and I hoped for the best. Much later, I read in George Weigel's book on the last years of the pontificate of John Paul II that my appointment to head the delegation had been "a break with tradition that rattled the Roman curia and the Holy See's Permanent Representative to the United Nations, Archbishop Renato Martino."[2]

One of the main aims of our group was to avert the situation that had developed at Cairo, where the abortion rights initiative championed by the United States had pushed all other conference issues into the background. There was reason to be optimistic. The idea that abortion was a legitimate tool of population control had been expressly rejected in the Cairo document, and in the months leading up to the Beijing conference, it seemed that most nations had little disposition to reopen the matter. The United States, moreover, was now unlikely to take the lead on any controversial issue. Not only had the Clinton administration been chastened by the preceding year's elections, in which the Republican Party had captured control of Congress for the first time since 1952, but the Senate had adopted a bipartisan resolution instructing the U.S. delegates to Beijing not to denigrate motherhood and the family.

The Holy See's positions on the conference topic, "Action for Equality, Development, and Peace," were grounded in the Church's teachings on social and economic justice, and we stood a good chance of being heard, if only the conference would stay focused on those areas. Our hopes were dimmed, however, by the fact that the preparatory document produced for the conference by the UN Commission on the Status of Women was a poorly written, 149-pages-single-spaced hodgepodge of ideas. Population-control lobbyists and old-line, hard-line feminist groups had heavily influenced the drafting process, and a large proportion of the document was left in brackets, signifying that no accord could be reached on a number of items. A host of knotty problems were thus left to be worked out in China.

The draft document, from our delegation's point of view, was deeply flawed. Many provisions addressed issues of equal opportunity, education, and development in a sensible way. But, remarkably, they showed no recognition that most women in the world marry and most have children. The implicit vision of women's progress was based on the model, increasingly challenged by men and women alike, in which family responsibilities are avoided or subordinated to personal advancement. When dealing with health, education, and young girls, the drafts emphasized sex and reproduction to the neglect of many other crucial issues.

The conference began with a colorful opening ceremony organized by the Chinese government in the Great Hall of the People. Like the conference document, it was an odd mixture. There were mistresses of ceremonies in sequined gowns, accomplished ballet dancers, gyrating hula-hula girls, and models sporting the latest fashions. A performance by the Beijing Women's Philharmonic Orchestra was followed by a martial arts display where the women vanquished all the men.

As soon as the curtain fell, our delegation went into action. Some worked day and night in negotiating sessions to make the conference documents more responsive to the actual lives of women, and some reached out to make common cause with other delegations where possible, while others liaised with NGOs. Two exceptionally capable American monsignors (now bishops), Frank Dewane and David Malloy, brought invaluable experience from the previous year's population conference in Cairo. Navarro and American journalist Joan Lewis, who was part of our delegation, handled relations with the press. Every evening we met in our Holiday Inn headquarters for Mass and discussion of the day's events.

One of the most impressive speakers at the conference was Pakistani Prime Minister Benazir Bhutto, who zeroed in on some of the defects in the preparatory documents. They were, she said, "disturbingly weak" on the role of the traditional family and on the connection between family disintegration and general moral decay. Similarities between the positions of the Holy See delegation and representatives from majority-Muslim countries on certain issues prompted the press to speak of an "unholy alliance," but we were so far apart from them on women's equality that our contacts were limited to formal greetings.

When Hillary Clinton, then first lady, took the podium, it was apparent that the American administration's strategy had undergone a sea change since Cairo. In a cautiously worded speech, Mrs. Clinton condemned direct coercion in population-control programs and made several positive references to women's roles as mothers and family members. She did, however, take the occasion to lift up the misleading slogan "Human rights are women's rights and women's rights are human rights." The statement was half true. Human rights are women's rights—they belong to everyone, everywhere. But not everything that has been called a woman's right in one or more countries is recognized as a universal human right.

In my opening statement to the conference, I reaffirmed the positions the Holy See had taken at Cairo, and I called attention to several areas where the Beijing drafts needed to be improved. The documents barely mentioned marriage, motherhood, and the family except negatively as impediments to women's self-realization (and as associated with violence and oppression). The women's health section focused disproportionately on sexual and reproductive matters, with scarcely a glance toward primary health care, nutrition, sanitation, tropical diseases, access to basic services, or even maternal morbidity and mortality. Women's poverty was addressed in narrow terms as chiefly a problem of equality between women and men, slighting the influence of family breakdown and economic structures. I pointed out that, without recognition and support of women's roles in child raising, effective equality would remain elusive for far too many. I concluded with the observation that there can be no real progress for women, or men, at the expense of children or of the underprivileged. These points seemed so reasonable to us that, in the first few days of the conference, we were confident they would find wide support.

Ominous signs, however, soon appeared. Some delegations from developing countries arrived at sessions involving sexual and reproductive matters with position papers that were identical to one another and whose language resembled the statements of Western abortion rights groups. Our own negotiators were getting rough treatment from chairpersons wielding heavy gavels, especially in sessions dealing with the controversial health sections of the draft.

By the end of the first week, it was clear that a coalition led by the European Union had taken up leadership on the sexual and abortion rights front. Negotiating as a bloc, they were pushing hard on a version of the agenda that had been rejected by the Cairo conference. And their efforts were so aggressive that negotiators were failing to make progress on any other issues.

From the beginning, two aspects of the behavior of the European negotiators struck me as very odd. First, many of their positions contradicted well-established principles in their own national laws and constitutions. Second, they were opposing references to key international human rights principles to which their own governments had subscribed, such as Article 16 of the Universal Declaration of Human Rights (UDHR), which provides that "the family is the natural and fundamental group unit of society and is entitled to protection by society and the state."

The EU group's indifference to basic principles of international human rights seemed to have no bounds. They contested every effort to include the word *motherhood* in the conference documents except where it appeared in a negative light, even though the Universal Declaration and many European laws provided that "motherhood and childhood are entitled to special care and assistance" (Art. 25). They objected to a paragraph providing for freedom of conscience and religion in the context of education, in spite of the UDHR's provision that "everyone has the right to freedom of thought, conscience, and religion . . . [including] freedom, either alone or in community with others and in public or private, to manifest his religion or belief in teaching, practice, worship, and observance" (Art. 18). And they sought to eliminate all recognition of parental rights and duties from the draft in defiance of UDHR Article 26, which gives parents the "prior right to choose the education of their children."

The EU negotiators' behavior was a prime example of a phenomenon I had criticized in *Rights Talk*—the tendency when arguing for a favorite right to brush aside all other rights and obligations.

By the end of the first week of the conference, the European coalition's relentless focus on sexual and reproductive rights had brought progress on other issues to a near standstill. So that Friday night, Diarmuid Martin, Navarro, and I composed a press release raising the question of whether the EU negotiators were exceeding their authority. We faxed it to all the major European newspapers and waited.

By Monday, there was a marked change in the negotiating atmosphere. Questions had begun to be posed in European legislatures, including the EU Parliament, concerning what their delegations were up to in Beijing. One of our negotiators reported that an unhappy EU delegate complained to her, "Why did you people have to bring all this out in the open?"

Negotiations began moving again, and the final documents that were taking shape, section by section, in different negotiating rooms, began to look like something the Holy See might accept, at least in part.

By the time the conference drew to a close, the conference documents had been improved in many ways, but the picture was mixed.

A number of considerations weighed in favor of the documents. The principle that abortion must not be promoted as a method of family planning had been reaffirmed. The provisions in the program of action that were closest to the themes of the conference—equality, development, and peace—were also the most consistent with Catholic teachings on dignity, freedom, and social justice. These included sections dealing with the needs of women in poverty, and with strategies for development, literacy, and education; for ending violence against women; for building a culture of peace; and for providing access for women to employment, land, capital, and technology. We could also support general statements on the connection between the feminization of poverty and family disintegration, the discrimination against women that begins with abortion of unborn females, and the promotion of partnership and mutual respect between men and women. Moreover, many of those ideas—such as the emphasis on women's education and the insistence that the human person must be at the center of concern in development—had been introduced by (or with the help of) the Holy See over the years. Aided by the Friday night press release, our negotiators even succeeded in securing references to relevant universal rights and obligations in areas where those principles had been deliberately ignored.

But the documents still had serious defects. They were weaker on parental rights and respect for religious and cultural values than the Cairo documents had been, and although EU efforts to include the phrase "sexual rights" were rebuffed, the final documents did contain ambiguous rights language in the areas of sexuality and fertility. There was no consensus on what this vague new language meant, but our delegation was concerned that vague language on sexual and reproductive "health" would be used to promote the agendas of aggressive population-control groups who were indifferent to the beliefs, hopes, and capacity for self-determination of those whose reproductive behavior they wished to control.

Much of the foundation money that swirled around the Beijing process was aimed at forging a link between development aid and programs that pressured poor women into abortion, sterilization, and the use of risky contraceptive methods. Disregarding abundant evidence that economic development and women's education lead to lowered fertility rates, these groups wanted population control on the cheap.

The Holy See's position was thus a difficult one—one that Catholic laypeople often face when they enter the messy world of politics. When does political compromise become moral compromise?

Earlier that year, Pope John Paul II had given important guidance to Catholic elected officials on whether, in cases where it is not possible to overturn a pro-abortion law, one can legitimately "support proposals aimed at limiting the harm done by such a law and at lessening its negative consequences at the level of general opinion and public morality" (*Evangelium Vitae,* 73). To vote for such a law, the pope said, "does not in fact represent an illicit cooperation with an unjust law, but rather a legitimate and proper attempt to limit its evil aspects."

Though relevant to our decision at Beijing, that advice left it up to decision makers to make prudential judgments about how to mitigate negative consequences under each circumstance. Should the Holy See as a moral witness on the world stage entirely repudiate the flawed conference declaration and program of action? Or would it be more effective to join in consensus on the good parts, and to witness to the truth at the same time by explaining our reasons for rejecting the parts that were injurious to women and to human dignity?

After an intense discussion in which members of our delegation shared their views, hopes, doubts, and concerns about the documents, we were divided. Some members of the group, including Archbishop Martino, advocated that we walk out of the conference, while others, including me, suggested that the Holy See would do more good by associating with the best parts of the documents and entering formal reservations to the parts that it could not accept. The decision would have to be made by the pope himself.

I placed a call to Archbishop Jean-Louis Tauran, the wise French diplomat who was serving as the foreign minister of the Holy See (Secretary for Relations with States). I gave him my assessment of the pros and cons of various courses of actions, stating my own preference. While awaiting his report on the pope's decision, I wrote two speeches: one partially associating the Holy See with the conference consensus, and the other explaining our inability to join the consensus at all. The exercise was reminiscent of my most terrifying law school class, where Karl Llewellyn had given us students an actual trial record and required us to be prepared when called upon to make an appellate argument for either side.

After hours of nervous waiting, I heard from Archbishop Tauran. The pope had said: "Accept what you can, and vigorously reject what cannot be accepted."

I was immensely relieved.

The Holy See associated itself in part with the conference documents, making several reservations. I began my announcement of our position by quoting the eloquent words of John Paul II on women's quest for equality in his June 1995 letter to women: "When one looks at the great process of women's liberation, the journey has been a difficult and complicated one and, at times, not without its share of mistakes.

But it has been substantially a positive one, even if it is still unfinished, due to the many obstacles which, in various parts of the world, still prevent women from being acknowledged, respected, and appreciated in their own special dignity. This journey must go on!"

In keeping with the Holy Father's instructions, I praised the parts of the documents that were conducive to women's flourishing, and I was sharply critical of the deficiencies that our delegation had tried from the beginning to publicize and remedy. In addition to our reservations, we attached a "statement of interpretation" on the word *gender*. During the conference, a controversy over the word had been largely defused with a consensus that it was to be understood according to ordinary usage in the United Nations context. But the final Beijing documents were still permeated with that ambiguous word. So, out of prudence, the Holy See explicitly dissociated itself from the notion that sexual identity is merely a malleable social construct. But we also made it clear that the Holy See rejected any crude form of biological determinism. In this we were mindful of the pope's writings to and about women where he acknowledged that we do not know everything there is to know about what is natural and what is cultural in men and women.

In the end, the Beijing conference did not reach a solid consensus. The Holy See was among an unusually large number of UN members, 43 of 181 present, that dissented from parts of the conference documents. One lesson I took away from that rowdy conference was that huge international gatherings are not suitable settings for addressing complex questions of social and economic justice or grave issues of human rights.

I returned to Harvard thinking that at least the Holy See could feel proud that it had amplified the voices of women whose concerns would otherwise have been sidelined. The Holy See was the only entity at the Beijing conference whose sphere of concern, like that of the UN, was worldwide. With over three hundred thousand educational, health care, and relief agencies serving mainly the poor in every region on the planet, it had a wealth of firsthand experience in ministering to the most basic needs of women and girls. We had called attention to the plight of women who lacked adequate primary health care, nutrition, and sanitation (all of which were given short shrift due to the conference's fixation on reproductive health). And we had responded to what we believed was the desire of most women everywhere for a feminism that is not hostile to men, marriage, and motherhood—a feminism that treats men and women as equal partners on their journey through life.

A month after the Beijing conference, Pope John Paul II came to the United States to deliver an address on the occasion of the fiftieth anniversary of the United Nations. After the speech, at a reception organized by Archbishop Martino (then the Holy See's permanent observer at the United Nations), Navarro came up to me and asked, "Where were you last night? You were supposed to have dinner at the archbishop's residence with the pope. He wanted to thank you in person for Beijing." I had not been invited. Apparently, Archbishop Martino had "forgotten" the pope's request that I be present.

That incident was disappointing, not only because I would have liked to have been there, but because I still had a rather romanticized view of the priesthood. I hoped the archbishop had just made a mistake. Later I read in George Weigel's personal reminiscences about the papacy of John Paul II, *Lessons in Hope,* that many curial prelates in those days were still in shock at the demise of the Italian papacy and resented the presence of *stranieri,* foreigners, in the Vatican. Even Navarro, a Spaniard, had once heard Secretary of State Cardinal Sodano say that "foreigners don't fit in well here." Perhaps a female foreigner was too much for Martino to bear.

The Vatican is a small place, however, and Martino's and my paths continued to cross now and then. Years later, when I was U.S. Ambassador to the Holy See, I invited Martino, then a cardinal and head of the Pontifical Council for Pastoral Care of Migrants and Itinerant People, to be a panelist at an embassy conference. He arrived all warmth and smiles and opened his talk with words of praise for my leadership at Beijing. It had been his idea, he told the audience, that I should be the first woman to head a Holy See delegation!

A few days after John Paul II's UN speech, Navarro emailed me to say that the pope wanted to have dinner with me when I was next in Rome. He added that my daughter Elizabeth, an art historian living in Rome, would be welcome as well. A date was arranged and that November, Diarmuid Martin met Liz and me at the Bronze Doors and escorted us to the papal apartments on the third floor of the Apostolic Palace.

Liz, having guided many visitors through the splendors of Saint Peter's Basilica and the Vatican Museum, had hoped we might see a rare painting or two. But we were both struck by the austerity of the pope's quarters. The only items on display in the entryway were simple handmade gifts the pope had received from various parts of the world.

After a short wait, we were greeted by the Holy Father himself and his secretary, then Monsignor Stanisław Dziwisz, who led us into a small dining room where we were joined by then Bishop Stanisław Ryłko. Dziwisz and Ryłko were two of the pope's oldest and closest associates from his days as Archbishop of Cracow. On the way to the apartments, Diarmuid had told me that the pope would throw out a few questions and expect the rest of us to do most of the talking. When I saw there were no other guests, I realized that this probably meant I was on the spot.

Sure enough, the Holy Father opened the conversation by asking me what I thought the "new feminism" that he had called for should look like. I began by telling him about Women Affirming Life, a group that I and other Catholic women had founded in Boston with the motto "Pro-life, Pro-woman, Pro-child, Pro-poor." That conversation continued through dinner, with Elizabeth, the affable Polish prelates, and Diarmuid chiming in. The pope said little, but he smiled in apparent approval. It felt like a family dinner, except for the food.

I doubt that anyone in Rome had a more spartan meal than we were served that evening. The first course, a clear broth with a few noodles, was followed by a thin slice of meat, a couple of carrots, and a small boiled potato. Dessert was a few slices of fruit with a bit of cheese. Afterward, when Liz and I were standing alone in the Piazza San Pietro, we looked at each other for a minute and then headed over to the Borgo Pio for a plate of pasta.

My experiences in Beijing prompted me to reflect on how challenging it is to try to live up to the role of the laity as envisioned by Vatican II, not only to bring Christian principles into the secular sphere where we live and work, but also to

enter the messy and morally risky realm of politics when circumstances permit. I like to think that the work of our mostly
lay delegation helped to encourage other lay Catholics to take
the plunge.

The Beijing experience also deepened my already profound appreciation for the remarkable pontificate of Pope
John Paul II. His instruction to the Holy See delegation to
"be a voice for the voiceless" was illustrative of the dramatic
shift he had effected in Vatican diplomacy when he became
pope in 1978. Under Popes John XXIII and Paul VI, Holy
See diplomats had refrained from open criticism of regimes
behind the iron curtain, believing that to be the best way of
protecting the Church in those countries. John Paul II, however, regarded the Church's primary role in the public square
to be that of a clear and consistent moral witness. Under his
pontificate, the Holy See became a leading champion of fundamental human rights.

The philosopher-pope's decision on how to deal with the
flawed Beijing conference documents was illustrative of another characteristic of his pontificate. It was a practical appli-
cation of his general approach to the promise and perils of our
time: discerning and building on the positive elements of the
prevailing culture, while naming and countering what is false
and harmful. As he put it later that fall during his visit to the
United States, "Sometimes, witnessing to Christ will mean
drawing out of a culture the full meaning of its noblest inten-
tions, a fullness that is revealed in Christ. At other times, witnessing to Christ means challenging that culture, especially
when the truth about the human person is under assault."

CHAPTER THREE

Getting to Know the Curia

✤

*Curia: In European medieval history, a court, or group of
persons who attended a ruler at any given time for social,
political, or judicial purposes.*

—ENCYCLOPAEDIA BRITANNICA

"The first thing to understand about the Vatican," an Italian
friend once told me, "is that it is a court." The Roman curia,
the central administrative body that assists the pope in governing the affairs of the Catholic Church, is often referred to
as the Holy See's bureaucracy. And with its secretariats, congregations, councils, commissions, academies, tribunals, and
other offices, the curia does bear some resemblance to the bureaucracies of modern governments. But my friend was right.
The Roman curia, headed by one man with supreme authority, is what its name says it is: a court. And it is a most unusual
court, with many lords and few ladies, and whose chief responsibility is the care of souls and spreading the good news
of salvation throughout the world.

Central Committee for the Great Jubilee 2000

My introduction to that little world behind the walls of Vatican City took place in 1994, a year before the Beijing conference, when I was appointed to the Central Committee for the
Great Jubilee 2000. All I knew about the Jubilee Committee

was that Pope John Paul II had established it in his apostolic letter *Tertio Millennio Adveniente,* "As the Third Millennium Approaches," which he issued to "suggest courses of reflection and action" as the Church prepared for the beginning of the third millennium.

As the committee's work progressed, I learned that John Paul II had attached high importance to the anniversary of the birth of Jesus Christ from the beginning of his pontificate. On the day of his election as pope in 1978, his revered mentor Cardinal Stefan Wyszynski, the primate of Poland, had taken him aside and told him, "You are to lead the Church into the third millennium." A year later, in his first encyclical, *Redemptor Hominis,* "The Redeemer of Man," the new pope spoke of the need to prepare for a "new Advent" in the final years of the second millennium. In *Tertio Millennio Adveniente,* he said that "preparing for the *Year 2000 has become as it were a hermeneutical key of my Pontificate*" (emphasis in original).

Tertio Millennio Adveniente also emphasized the link between the Jubilee and the Second Vatican Council. It was in the council, the pope said, where preparations for the jubilee year were "really begun." That meant, he added, that "the best preparation for the new millennium can only be expressed in a renewed commitment *to apply,* as faithfully as possible, *the teachings of Vatican II to the life of every individual and of the whole Church*" (emphasis in original). The jubilee should mark a commitment toward "a new springtime of Christian life."

The committee would thus be required to ground its work in the teachings of Vatican II and to examine the present situation of the Church in the light of the pope's encyclicals elaborating on those teachings. It seemed like a tall order. When I arrived in the Vatican for the first meeting of the Jubilee Committee, the group's secretary general greeted me and said, "Your speech will be at 11:15." That was a surprise, as nothing had been mentioned about a speech in our correspondence. I had given some thought to what I might contribute to the discussions, and I did have an idea or two that I was hoping to present at some point after I had gotten a sense of the group. But I was hardly prepared to give a speech and more than a little awed when I saw who else was in the room.

The thirty-two members of the committee were seated around a long rectangular table. It was an imposing display of crimson and magenta. At the head of the table was the president, Cardinal Roger Etchegaray, a tall, rough-hewn Basque who had served as a papal negotiator in some of the world's most dangerous and troubled places, courageously remaining at his post in the aftermath of the Rwandan civil war when other foreigners were fleeing. He was a man who always looked most at home in his plain black clericals, and who unapologetically spoke French with a bit of a regional accent. Cardinal Etchegaray was flanked by two other great churchmen, Cardinal Camillo Ruini, the scholarly, bespectacled Vicar General for the Diocese of Rome, and Cardinal Francis Arinze, a Nigerian cleric whose visible happiness in his vocation was a joy to behold and who was heading the Pontifical Council for Interreligious Dialogue. In my interactions with each of those three very different men over the years, I always felt I was in the presence of a prelate who was first and foremost a priest.

Along the sides of the table, archbishops, bishops, monsignors, and priests were seated in order of precedence. I was happy to see Diarmuid Martin's familiar face among them. At the farthest end of the table were the three women members: Sister Klara Sietmann, the president of the International Union of Superiors General, a tall imposing German; Marie-Ange Besson, whom I knew from the Pontifical Council for Justice and Peace; and me. Besides Marie-Ange and me, there was only one other layperson on the committee, the national president of the Italian Sports Centre, Professor Donato Mosella, who was seated with the monsignors.

After making some welcoming remarks, Cardinal Etchegaray called upon the members to introduce themselves and offer comments. As the comments proceeded, I realized with immense relief that my "speech" could be short. When my turn came, I suggested that the Jubilee Year would be an ideal occasion to send a message to lapsed or estranged Catholics. In order to reach so many people who were outside the Church's ordinary methods of communication, I said that some attention-getting symbol would be needed. So I proposed placing a "Jubilee lamp" in front of every Catholic church, a light burning night and day for the entire year leading up to the year 2000. Its message to the Church's absent children would be something like "We're thinking about you here at home, we miss you, please come in and talk." My suggestion went nowhere, but it has been heartening in recent years to see Catholic churches here and there taking steps to beckon the wanderers back home.

Among the prelates who spoke that day, one suggested a contest for designing a jubilee logo, another proposed a special prayer for the occasion, and many discussed the pros and cons of having some expression of repentance by the pope for sins committed by members of the Church.

An intervention by the German sister made the ecclesiastical heads turn. Reminding everyone present that her association represented over half a million women religious in eighty countries around the world, she said that she would have to report to her fellow superiors general on precisely what her role on this committee was to be. What, she asked, was the significance of a seating arrangement that placed the women at the end of the table? And were the women to have a real part in the planning process? If not, she indicated that she had other things to do.

The seating arrangements, except for the inclusion of Mosella among the monsignors, were in order of rank within the Vatican, but the fact that the women were few and placed at the table's end illustrated aspects of ecclesiastical culture that grated on women who (like Sister Klara, I imagine) had often been made to feel marginalized. In any case, the optics were not ideal for a group that was supposed to deliberate on how the Church ought to enter the third millennium.

At the next meeting, the seating arrangement was changed. The German sister, however, never came back. For the rest of the committee's existence, I was seated next to Francesco Marchisano, a gentlemanly archbishop from the Piedmont region, who became a good friend. He had two sisters of whom he was very fond and, like the pope, he was quite at ease with women. At one meeting, he whispered to me that he looked forward to the day when women were represented in the Church "at the highest levels." Not for the first time, it occurred to me that it was a great gift for a priest to have siblings, nieces, and nephews—both in terms of personal happiness and in their general outlook on life.

The committee spent most of its time discussing logistical

and ceremonial matters without much dissent, but one sensitive subject was the pope's call for the Church to be penitent for aspects of its past. Specifically, some members of the committee had reservations concerning expressions of sorrow for errors or misdeeds on the part of representatives of the Church at various times in history. In fact, that issue turned out to be the single most controversial aspect of the preparation for the jubilee so far as the Church hierarchy was concerned.

There was no doubt where Pope John Paul II stood on the matter. In *Tertio Millennio Adveniente,* he had already called for a broad examination of conscience as the third Christian millennium approached. The Church, he said, "is always holy because of her incorporation in Christ," but she is "always in need of being purified, and thus never tires of repenting." Over the remaining years of the twentieth century, there were a number of instances—one journalist counted ninety-four—where the pope acknowledged the mistakes and sins of Christians in connection with the Crusades, the Inquisition, the treatment of Jews, religious wars, and the treatment of women. The Church, he announced, "approaches the twenty-first century on her knees."

Those papal apologies for historic wrongdoing were direct, to the point, and aimed toward what John Paul II sometimes called the "healing of memories." In every way, these apologies reflected the largeness of spirit that radiated from his writings and speeches. He reminded the faithful that "acknowledging the weaknesses of the past is an act of honesty and courage which helps to strengthen our faith, which alerts us to face today's temptations and challenges."

Those sentiments were never more movingly enacted than on John Paul's pilgrimage to Jerusalem in the Jubilee Year.

The pope, now elderly and infirm, slowly made his way down a long stone stairway to the Western Wall, the holiest place where Jews are permitted to pray. There, following the custom of pious Jews, he left a prayer in one of the wall's crevices. It read:

> *God of our fathers,*
> *you chose Abraham and his descendants*
> *to bring your Name to the Nations:*
> *we are deeply saddened by the behavior of those*
> *who in the course of history*
> *have caused these children of yours to suffer,*
> *and asking your forgiveness we wish to commit ourselves*
> *to genuine brotherhood*
> *with the people of the Covenant.*

My friend and fellow law professor Joseph Weiler was in Jerusalem, watching on television that day. He told me that he called his five children into the room to see the pope's gesture. "That," he told them, "is what Christians call a saint."

I supported the pope's expressions of sorrow, but I also sympathized with the committee members who were concerned about the way that his words could be manipulated by persons who wished to silence or discredit the voice of the Church—not to mention those for whom no apology would ever be enough, unless the Church apologized for its very existence. I feel sure that Pope John Paul was well aware that his words would be taken out of context and misused, but his conviction that preparation for the jubilee required an honest examination of conscience would not permit him to be silent.

In my view, the pope's decision to take those risks meant

that lay Catholics, in particular, should be vigilant and ready to rise to the Church's defense when she was unjustly maligned. I wrote an article for *First Things* magazine titled "Contrition in the Age of Spin Control," in which I warned that these apologies could be opportunistically exploited. "Expressions of sorrow over past shortcomings," I wrote, "do not require abasing ourselves before others, and certainly not before persons who are unwilling to admit any misdeeds of their own. . . . Let us make sure our expressions of sorrow are never permitted to denigrate the role of the Church in history as an overwhelmingly positive force for peace and justice."[3] The article, I regret to say, was prescient.

As a Catholic living in Boston in 2002, I was shocked and disgusted when the story broke about priestly sexual abuse of minors, and the horrifying revelations continued over the next several months. I was dismayed, however, by the misleading media coverage of the abuse scandal. Several in the media falsely implied that the Catholic Church was the main locus of child sexual abuse, when in actuality the problem pervades many institutions. There was scarcely a mention of the dreadful abuses and failures of supervision in public and private schools, other religious bodies, sports groups, and youth groups like the Boy Scouts.

It was only after a great deal of undeserved damage had been done to the reputations of Catholic priests and institutions that an important truth emerged. The John Jay College of Criminal Justice, after conducting two major studies on clergy sexual abuse for the U.S. Conference of Catholic Bishops, concluded that there were many institutions where abuse of minors was more common than in the Catholic Church, where supervisors covered it up, and where those in charge lagged behind the Church in acknowledging and addressing the problem. Yet "no organization has undertaken a study of itself in the manner of the Catholic Church."

Regardless of the disappointing media coverage, the Church's own introspection was unquestionably necessary. The unique trust placed in clergy, and the particular spiritual weight of their vocation, made the abuse especially egregious. That, together with the inaction of many clerics who knew of these misdeeds, placed the institutional Church in a credibility crisis. The same institution that runs hospitals, orphanages, and universities, and that provides humanitarian aid throughout the world, was also an institution where rogue clergy had sexually violated large numbers of children and adolescents. The challenge for the Church was to take full, unequivocal responsibility for grave evils while continuing to affirm its own existence. It was difficult to keep hold of the excruciating complexity of the crisis, in which many priests were denied due process, and to resist the temptation of simplistic analyses.

In retrospect, it seems to me that the Church leaders who did best in responding to the sex abuse crisis were those who took their bearings from John Paul II's insistence in the recently concluded jubilee on truth, humility, repentance, and healing. It was not easy, however, to put those principles into practice in the emotionally charged environment that surrounded these cases. The jubilee had ended on January 6, 2001, with the promulgation of a new apostolic letter, *Novo Millennio Ineunte,* "Entering the Third Millennium," in which the pope, perhaps with the emerging sex abuse crisis in mind, acknowledged that great challenges lay ahead.

Like its predecessor, *Tertio Millennio Adveniente,* the concluding letter stressed the importance of the teachings of the
Second Vatican Council: "With the passing of the years, *the
Council documents have lost nothing of their value or brilliance.*
They need to be read correctly, to be widely known and taken
to heart as important and normative texts of the Magisterium,
within the Church's Tradition" (emphasis in original). The
letter was forward-looking, urging the faithful to take up the
ever ancient, ever new challenge to witness to the good news
of Jesus Christ with renewed vigor. For that witness to be effective, the philosopher-pope emphasized another theme that
ran through his entire pontificate: the relationship between
faith and reason. "It is important," he wrote, "that special efforts be made to explain properly the reasons for the Church's
position, stressing that it is not a case of imposing on non-
believers a vision based on faith, but of interpreting and de-
fending the values rooted in the very nature of the human
person." Characteristically, John Paul II also insisted that "*the
laity* especially must be present" in the effort to bring the
Christian message to the twenty-first-century world (emphasis in original).

Pontifical Council for the Laity

Under the leadership of American Cardinal Francis Stafford,
the Pontifical Council for the Laity had participated enthusi-
astically in the preparations for the jubilee.

Created by Pope Paul VI in direct response to a proposal
of the Second Vatican Council, the purposes of the Pontifical
Council for the Laity were to promote the lay apostolate internationally, to provide advice to the hierarchy on matters

affecting the laity, to foster studies on the laity, to act as a clearinghouse for information, and to approve the statutes of new lay ecclesial movements. By its very existence, it symbolized Vatican II's recognition of the dignity of the laity and its promise of fostering a fuller participation of the laity in the apostolic life of the Church. It was unlike any other body in the curia in that lay members outnumbered members of the hierarchy and many of the lay members were women.

In fact, what surprised me most when the pope appointed me to the council in 1995 was that most of the members were leaders of lay movements like the Knights of Columbus, Focolare, the Neocatechumenate, Comunione e Liberazione, Opus Dei, the Community of Sant'Egidio, and other less well-known groups. Up to that time, I had never heard of most of these groups, even though their collective membership was in the millions.

One of this council's most popular and successful achievements had always been the organization of the World Youth Days, initiated by Pope John Paul II in 1985. And for the Jubilee 2000, the council pulled out all the stops. World Youth Day in the year 2000 was the largest pilgrimage in European history, drawing more than 2 million young men and women to Rome from all over the world. According to George Weigel, "In a year of spectacular displays of Catholic faith, this was perhaps the most stunning."

No doubt it also played a major role in advancing the new evangelization. It brought countless young people closer to the faith, and perhaps even helped to recatechize some of the worldly citizens of Rome. Few who were present will forget the pope's words to his young followers:

It is Jesus in fact that you seek when you dream of happiness; he is waiting for you when nothing else you find satisfies you; he is the beauty to which you are so attracted; it is he who provokes you with that thirst for fullness that will not let you settle for compromise; it is he who urges you to shed the masks of a false life; it is he who reads in your hearts your most genuine choices, the choices that others try to stifle. It is Jesus who stirs in you the desire to do something great with your lives, the will to follow an ideal, the refusal to allow yourselves to be ground down by mediocrity, the courage to commit yourselves humbly and patiently to improving yourselves and society, making the world more human and more fraternal.

The Synod for America

As part of the preparation for the Jubilee 2000, Pope John Paul II convened several gatherings of bishops from Africa, Europe, Asia, Oceania, and America to hear their views and gain their advice. In the fall of 1997, when the Synod for America took place, I was invited to be an auditor of the monthlong session. As I was a visiting professor at the Gregorian University in Rome that semester, it was easy to accept. The Synod for America brought bishops from all of America, north and south, to the Vatican to discuss the state of the Church in those regions and their role in the new evangelization.

On the eve of the synod, I had dinner near the Pantheon with my friends George Weigel and Father Richard Neuhaus. Richard, like me, would be attending the synod in an official capacity as a representative from the United States, while George was in Rome working on his magisterial biography of the pope. After dinner, we strolled over to the Church of Sant'Ignazio, where we listened to a choir performing the music of Palestrina and where Richard prayed at the tomb of Saint Robert Bellarmine.

The next morning, and every weekday for the month of November, I walked from my tiny garret near the Gregorian University across the Piazza della Rotonda and over the Tiber to the Vatican's Synod Hall, where 233 synod fathers, including forty cardinals, were assembled according to precedence in tiers of seats that sloped steeply upward. After the prelates came the priests, and after the priests came the auditors. Richard, who was used to presiding over many groups at home, was not entirely pleased at being in the very last row of the priests' section. I was seated directly behind him, in the front row of the auditors' section. From that lofty perch, we looked down on an ebony sea dotted with the crimson and magenta caps of prelates gathered from the northern reaches of Canada to the southernmost areas of Chile and Argentina.

I could not help noticing that Richard was always scribbling during the seemingly endless hours of speeches. It did not seem likely that he was taking notes. In fact, by the end of the synod, he had written a whole book, *Appointment in Rome: The Church in America Awakening.* In its preface, he wrote, "Not since that year in fourth grade under Miss Woodward have I experienced such tedium."

Each chair in the hall was equipped with a microphone, and every attendee was given an opportunity to speak. Simultaneous interpretation in English, French, Italian, Spanish, and Portuguese was provided. Each of the synod fathers was allotted eight minutes for his intervention, and the auditors were given six minutes each. As Richard assessed those meetings in his book:

> The hundreds of speeches pick and probe at pieces of problem and promise, but only episodically is there a statement that raises a coherent vision of what might be, and then it is quickly swamped by another deluge of unrelated homilies, complaints, and exhortations to do—well, to do something.

Mother Mary Quentin Sheridan, then secretary of the Council of Major Superiors of Women Religious, a diminutive woman of formidable energy, intellect, and good cheer, made one of the more memorable interventions. Like Catherine of Siena exhorting the popes of old, she reminded the clergy that, while they are teaching, sanctifying, and governing, they are acting "in the person of Christ!" The only crisis of the priesthood, she said, was the crisis of priests and bishops who do not understand the incredible gift and responsibility that is theirs. The listeners gave her prolonged applause. Later, when asked by a friend what she had said to the group, she reportedly replied, "I told them to act like men!"

About half of the synod participants were Latin American prelates. For me it was unsettling that so many of their remarks were focused on the United States—some blaming the U.S. for their problems, others contending that the U.S. should intervene to solve their problems, and many doing both. Those interventions were a preview of attitudes that became more prevalent in the Vatican during the pontificate of Pope Francis.

I devoted most of my six minutes to suggestions for healing the breach between Catholic conservatives and liberals, a topic that was much on my mind as a member of the Catholic Common Ground Initiative established the previous year by Chicago Cardinal Joseph Bernardin.

Although the synod's plenary sessions were entirely devoted to prepared statements by the participants, there was plenty of opportunity for discussion in the small working groups to which each of us was assigned by primary language, and even livelier exchanges occurred during coffee breaks, when little language groups tended to form. Some multilingual prelates worked the room during those breaks, moving from group to group. Language facility is a great asset in such environments, and no doubt is a factor that goes into the selection of a pope.

Though Pope John Paul II was frail, he presided over meetings that ran each weekday from nine o'clock in the morning to half past noon, and then again from five to seven o'clock in the evening. The long breaks were a boon for me, enabling me to go back to the Gregorian for my class and meetings with students. But it was a grueling schedule for the pope. He sometimes nodded off, but so did many in the audience.

Ever eager to hear views from many sources, the pope hosted a number of lunches and dinners for small groups of synod participants. I thus found myself at a table in the Apostolic Palace for a "francophone" evening with a handful of prelates who were more comfortable with French than English or Italian, including the general secretary of the synod, Cardinal Schotte, and Father Peter Hans Kolvenbach, who was then the Superior General of the Jesuits and who was known as the "Black Pope" because of the plain black cassock traditionally worn by members of that order. Having spent several years teaching at Boston College, where I had many Jesuit colleagues, I was interested to hear Father Kolvenbach observe that the Catholic character of many originally Catholic institutions of higher education was "probably irretrievably lost."

When the Holy Father greeted me, I mentioned that I had taught a class that morning on *Sollicitudo Rei Socialis,* "On Social Concern," the 1987 encyclical on which Schotte had lectured to the Social Justice Committee in Boston. That encyclical had met a cool reception among economically conservative Catholics in the United States, but I admired its extended reflection on the concept of solidarity, a subject close to the heart of the Polish pope. "I wish I had been there," he said. *So do I,* I thought, recalling the lively class discussion during which some of the Gregorian students had claimed that *Sollicitudo* was overly influenced by leftists in the Pontifical Council for Justice and Peace.

When the party was seated around the table, Cardinal Schotte began the conversation by saying, "The Holy Father tells me that he is currently rereading all of his encyclicals. Isn't that so, Your Holiness?" The pope, with a twinkle in his eye, replied, "Yes, at least the parts that came from my own hand." That was a rather mischievous remark since Schotte had assisted with the preparation of several papal documents. In fact, we now know that much of the work on *Sollicitudo* was done in the Council for Justice and Peace, where Schotte was secretary at the time. The document is said to have had more input from others than any of John Paul II's previous encyclicals, but the principal author's distinctive voice does ring out at key points.

Edward Meets the Pope

When I next saw the pope, a year later, his struggle with in-firmity was painfully evident. Edward and I had been in Bel-gium, visiting our friends Michel and Marie-Thérèse Meulders of the Louvain medical and law faculties, respec-tively, when another friend, the Catholic social philosopher Michael Novak, called. "Come to Rome tomorrow," he in-sisted. "We're having dinner with the Holy Father." At last, my Jewish husband would meet the pope whom he so ad-mired and whose love for "our elder brothers in the faith" he so appreciated.

Pope John Paul greeted Edward with great warmth, clasp-ing my husband's hands in his. Advancing Parkinson's dis-ease had made it ever more difficult for him to engage in conversation, but he urged Michael to expand on a knotty problem mentioned in *Centesimus Annus,* "The Hundredth Year," an encyclical written in 1991 on the anniversary of the founding encyclical of Catholic social teaching, *Rerum No-varum,* "Of New Things." The problem the pope asked Mi-chael to reflect on was how to discipline, without stifling, the creative energies of the market. And he seemed to enjoy the friendly back-and-forth between Michael, a theological and moral advocate of capitalism, and my liberal Democratic hus-band.

Edward's favorite memory of that dinner was seeing the pope tuck his napkin into his collar. That was a practice I had sometimes discouraged at home, but from the way Edward glanced at me across the table, I realized the issue was now settled once and for all. The food was meager that evening. The Polish nuns charged with caring for the Holy Father now had him on a diet that was even more austere than when Liz and I had dined with him three years earlier. But the pope's eyes lit up when we were served three small pieces of cheese for dessert. After finishing every bit, he licked his knife. Again, I got a meaningful look from my husband. Another admonition would never be repeated in the Glendon-Lev household.

The jury will long be out on whether and to what extent Jubilee 2000 shifted probabilities toward Pope John Paul's dream of a reinvigorated Church whose presence would be more meaningful in a world that had profoundly changed since Vatican II. The emphasis on repentance for sins of the past and the effects of World Youth Day 2000 on a generation of young men and women are regarded by many as the jubilee's most memorable contributions. But the synod process was also marked by a number of disagreements that have intensified over the years. One issue that occasionally surfaced but received relatively little attention in jubilee discussions involved the status of women in the Church.

I was, of course, aware that there was much discontent with Church leadership on the part of many women, and that much of it related to "decision-making power." One of these women was my cousin Barbara Glendon. We had grown up together in Dalton and remained close until shortly after her graduation from college, when she surprised all her relatives by sending us a kind of farewell letter announcing her entry into the Ursuline religious order and informing us that her new name would be Sister John Mary Vianney, a name taken after the sainted "Curé d'Ars." In those days, the strict rules of the Ursulines meant that she would not see her parents for

a very long time. Even family phone calls were quite restricted.

For several years, Barbara taught mathematics in an Ursuline school for girls. Later, as rules relaxed, she became an
activist for social justice, exchanged her traditional religious
habit for a pantsuit, moved into an apartment, bought single
shares in various corporations so that she could protest their
activities in stockholder meetings, and changed her name
back to Barbara. I thought Barbara would be pleased when I
told her about the Holy See delegation to the Beijing Wom-
en's Conference. But instead she said, "Mary Ann, I hope
you do realize that the institutional church is totally irrele-
vant."

From our encounters over the years at meetings of the
Catholic Common Ground Initiative, I learned that Barbara's dismissive attitude toward "the institutional church" was
bound up to some extent with her embrace of an angry feminism of the 1970s. But I could never presume to judge her.
When I visited my prickly cousin in her agonizing final illness, I found her with a world atlas on her bed, open to Africa. She was offering up each day's suffering for the poor,
hungry, and ailing of that continent, choosing a different
country every morning. She had given her entire life to
Christ, while I merely gave speeches, wrote papers, and went
back home to a loving husband, three wonderful daughters,
and satisfying work.

My sympathies for Barbara, for women religious, and for
laywomen who work for Church entities only increased as I
learned more about their experiences. I wish Barbara had
lived to see how many of a new generation of priests, espe-

cially those accustomed to coeducation, have taken to heart the forceful messages of John Paul II on the dignity of women.

A young Paulist sister from Boston told me a touching story that captures a good deal about John Paul's sensitivities to individuals—men and women, young and old. She had been invited to attend a small private Mass in the pope's chapel, and afterward, as she stood in line to be greeted by him, she became very nervous. When the pope appeared in front of her, she was so overwhelmed by emotion that all she could say was "I love you, Holy Father." The pope shook his finger at her, and said in a joking way, "No, it is forbidden to love the Holy Father." But as he moved down the line, he must have rethought his response. He stopped, returned to where she was standing, bent down, and kissed her forehead.

CHAPTER FOUR

Inside a Vatican Think Tank

✤

The best laid schemes o' Mice an' Men
gang aft agley.

—ROBERT BURNS, "To a Mouse"

By 1994 Pope John Paul II, as a major contributor to Catholic social doctrine, was increasingly concerned with the need to keep the Church's social teaching abreast of changing social and economic conditions, and with the increasing difficulty of doing so. Even more than his predecessors, he consulted broadly with outside experts in the course of preparing his social encyclicals. And more than any other modern pope, he sought out and enjoyed hearing the ideas of persons with different perspectives, opinions, and faiths, and those with no faith. But over the years he came to believe that the Church needed more regular and extensive contact with the human sciences in order to make its own contributions effectively. With that goal in mind, he created alongside the four-hundred-year-old Pontifical Academy of Sciences a social science academy, the Pontifical Academy of Social Sciences (PASS).

He began his *motu proprio*—a personal edict by the pope, similar to an executive order—establishing the academy by giving credit to the many scholars and activists who had contributed to an impressive body of Catholic social thought in the past: "Over the last century the Church has strengthened her 'citizenship status' by perfecting her social doctrine . . . [in] close collaboration, on the one hand, with Catholic social movements, and on the other, with experts in the social sciences." But with the new millennium in mind, he declared that it was time to create a formal structure for this collaboration in order to meet the challenges of "the great tasks the future has in store." The academy's purpose was to promote "the study and progress of the social sciences, primarily economics, sociology, law and political science," and to offer the Church "elements which she can use in the development of her social doctrine."

It was a sign of Pope John Paul II's high hopes for the new academy that it was to share headquarters with the venerable science academy in the Casina Pio Quattro, an exquisite Renaissance villa situated in the Vatican gardens.

On the day of the first meeting in 1994, I asked the Roman taxi driver to take me all the way to the "casino," as the building was in a part of Vatican City that was unfamiliar to me. I didn't know why he cracked up when I mispronounced "casina" until I learned that "casino" can mean "brothel" or simply "a big mess."

The relatively small edifice, created as a summer residence for Pope Pius IV, is adorned with sixteenth-century frescoes, reliefs, and mosaics celebrating the Muses. The building opens out into an oval courtyard with a marble fountain at its center. Far from the horns and motors of Rome, shaded by Roman pines, with one large, well-equipped conference room, it was an ideal place for academic meetings.

I was impressed by the care that had been taken to ensure wide geographical representation reflective of the universality of the Catholic Church and the breadth of its concerns. The original thirty academicians were drawn from Africa, North and South America, Asia, Australia, and Eastern and Western Europe. Nearly all were leaders in economics, law, political science, or sociology.

There were some famous names: the Nobel Prize winner Kenneth Arrow, whose interests ranged far beyond economics; the German jurist Hans Zacher, who presided over all of that country's famed Max Planck Institutes; the rising Italian philosopher-statesman Rocco Buttiglione; and Hanna Suchocka, who had been the prime minister of Poland during the presidency of Lech Wałęsa. Not all were Catholics. After I got to know Kenneth Arrow, I asked him why he, a man of the Jewish faith who was much in demand elsewhere, had accepted the invitation to join the academy. He said he had been drawn by his admiration for John Paul II and by his appreciation of the worldwide humanitarian activities of the Catholic Church.

The pope opened the first meeting by outlining his expectations for us. He urged us not to regard our secluded meeting place as an enclave where scholars commune only with one another. We were to bring the wisdom of the social sciences to bear on human realities "with a view to finding solutions to people's concrete problems, solutions based on social justice." The relationship between Catholic social thought and the social sciences, he went on, should be a two-way street: the Church's social teachings not only should assimilate worthwhile ideas from the various disciplines but should help the social sciences open themselves to a broader horizon. The social sciences, he said, would be enriched by taking the spiritual nature of human beings into account and by attend-

ing to the deep human longings that transcend the merely
biological and material aspects of life.

A glance around the room, however, should have told anyone that it would not be easy to meet those expectations.
Communication across disciplinary boundaries is never simple, even among lawyers, economists, sociologists, and political scientists who share the same language and nationality.
Here was a group of men and women with very different
backgrounds and experiences and no common language. Simultaneous interpretation in five languages—English, Italian, French, German, Spanish—would be required. Nuances
would be lost. Misunderstandings would be inevitable.

The pope told us to search for "all the grains of truth present in the various intellectual and empirical approaches" of
the disciplines represented in our midst.[4] But the fact is that
those who are able to overcome the intellectual confines of
their own discipline are rare.

The academy's first president, Edmond Malinvaud, was a
courtly, reserved French gentleman who had often been
mentioned as a potential Nobel laureate for his contributions
to macroeconomic theory. He took his new responsibilities
very seriously, and it was evident that he had given a lot of
thought to identifying areas where there were gaps or ambi-
guities in the Church's social teaching, as well as areas where
changing circumstances required some further development.

After the pope departed, Malinvaud reminded us of what
we all knew very well about the current state of the social
sciences—that they were rife with disagreements, especially
where religion and morality were concerned, and that even
specialists had difficulty making accurate analyses and pre-
dictions. If we were to be useful to the Church, he said, we

should take care to explain our findings carefully, noting gaps and uncertainties, and "in particular, avoid thinking of ourselves as invested with a direct role in the formation of the social doctrine of the Church."

By the end of that first meeting, I could see already that the members had differing visions of the academy's role. Malinvaud, taking his guidance from the academy's statute and the pope's *motu proprio,* had emphasized that the group's work would be addressed primarily to the Holy See for possible use in the development of the Church's social teachings and secondarily to the international social science community. Some members, more politically inclined, did not understand, or did not wish to accept, that the Church's social teachings do not offer specific policy prescriptions. Or that the academy's purposes did not include making recommendations for the revision of Catholic doctrines on faith and morals. One member insisted that the academy should plunge right into the latter area with a view toward updating the teachings on human sexuality.

At the close of the three-day meeting, we decided to focus on three areas where we all agreed Catholic social thought was in need of development: the changing world of work; the dilemmas of democracy; and the changing age structure of society, which was placing strain on every country's capacity to provide for the needs of the very young, the elderly, and the severely ill and disabled.

For its first few years, the academy devoted most of its efforts to the topic of work and employment—the classic "social question" that had been treated by Leo XIII in the encyclical *Rerum Novarum* and by John Paul II's encyclical *Laborem Exercens*. It was a good choice. The field was rapidly changing, and practically everyone was willing and eager to contribute. The goal was to produce a book of reflections on that theme as the academy's contribution to the Church's celebration of Jubilee 2000.

My contribution, the first paper I presented to the academy, was delivered at the first plenary session on the work and employment theme. It was an essay on how the concept of a right to work, embodied in most of the world's constitutions, as well as in UN human rights documents, has been received and interpreted in various countries. I was particularly interested in the contrast between the United States and Western Europe. In the latter, a confluence of social democratic, Christian, Marxist, and feudal-paternalistic ideas had paved the way for the acceptance of social and economic rights in the wave of new constitution-making and international human rights activity that followed World War II. The United States, though endorsing the concept by approving the Universal Declaration of Human Rights, has never constitutionalized the idea of a right to work. The real question, I argued, is not whether the right is declared constitutional but which systems have done the best at maximizing their citizens' opportunities for employment.[5]

Over the course of that first meeting, the academicians began to get to know one another during breaks and over meals in the Casa Santa Marta, where we were lodged. The Casa, built during the pontificate of John Paul II, serves as a residence for some priests working in the Vatican and as a guesthouse for official visitors, and during papal conclaves it houses the cardinal-electors. The dorm atmosphere is conducive both to work and to collegiality. The rooms, though spartan, are all designed with workspaces, and there are meeting rooms on the ground floor where people can gather for conversation. As we interacted in those early days, it was already apparent to me that the academy's members had very different understandings of the purpose of the academy and of their roles in its work.

Two years into the work and employment project, Malinvaud had to say in his 1996 report to the pope that "the theme had been neither fully covered nor in sufficient depth"; insufficient attention had been paid to developing countries and the spiritual dimension of work; and plans for publication were complicated by the unlikelihood that any commercial publisher would be interested in a collection of papers of varying quality in several different languages.[6]

Two more years passed, and Malinvaud reported that the plan for a Jubilee 2000 volume had to be abandoned because, after three plenary sessions on work and employment, there were still too many "points which had not been addressed, or sufficiently addressed."[7] When Malinvaud told me he had given up on finding a publisher for the work that had been completed, I suggested that we turn the collection over to the Boston College labor law professor Thomas Kohler, who had been one of our invited experts and was willing to try to turn it into a publishable work. As pruned and edited by Kohler, it became a readable and useful contribution to the literature, and I was able to find an American publisher for it. It was published in 2003, nine years after the project began. In his introduction, Malinvaud wrote that both his own synthesis and the alternative opinion of another academician "have the substantial though not unanimous support of our academicians."[8] That one line spoke volumes about the state of the academy—and about the obstacles to John Paul II's vision for the development and role of Catholic social doctrine.

By then it should have been obvious that such a diverse group meeting for three or four days once or twice a year was not going to produce the kind of work the pope had hoped to see. At a minimum, that would have required a full-time academic director with a professional staff. But unlike learned academies in other countries, the PASS had no budget for research and no academic leadership on the premises. A part-time clerical chancellor had responsibility for purely administrative duties, and his task was "to assist the president." But as the only person other than clerical staff on the premises most of the time, he was tempted to exceed his statutory mandate.

After the human work project debacle, the academicians were impatient to move on to two other areas where Catholic social doctrine required *aggiornamento,* "updating": globalization and democracy. In *Centesimus Annus,* "The Hundredth Year," Pope John Paul II had praised liberal democracy for its commitment to the protection of human freedom and dignity, its structural limits on the abuse of power, and its impressive resources for self-correction. And he acknowledged the free market's capacity to foster creativity, stimulate economic growth, and enable people to build a better future for themselves and their families. But he had cautioned that both democratic government and the free market needed a strong juridical framework, undergirded by a healthy moral culture, if they were to function for the common good.

Both projects began well with strong leadership, but as time went on, both projects ran into difficulties similar to those that had bedeviled the project on labor and employment. Members with differing academic specialties and contrary political views could not agree on how the work should proceed. Moreover, since all the academicians were busy people serving on a volunteer basis, it was hard for many of them to make the time commitment necessary for high-quality work. Meetings or workshops once or twice a year in Rome were never long enough to work out differences and reach consensus. Sometimes the most vocal members at meetings had the least expertise in the subject matter and had spent the least time on the project. Not surprisingly, Malinvaud's report to the pope in 2000 sounded more than a mild note of frustration. The members had been unable to agree on the program for the following year's plenary session, which was supposed to be devoted to globalization.[9]

The democracy project ran into difficulties as well. After a workshop and two plenary meetings devoted to the subject, Hans Zacher, its director, reported that "despite all these endeavors to relate the academy's discussion of democracy to the social teaching of the Church, the results clearly need further research and debate."[10] Two years later, Malinvaud reported that some members (surely including himself) had concerns about lack of rigor in much of the academy's work. They were stressing the need to move from descriptions to explanations, and complaining that plenary discussions were often terminated before differences had been identified or clear conclusions drawn.[11]

It was time to face the fact that the academy did not possess within its ranks sufficient expertise to deal comprehensively with topics as broad and complex as globalization and democracy. Zacher therefore proposed that external experts on

Catholic social thought should be called in to evaluate what had been done thus far with a view toward identifying what contribution the academy could make to the social doctrine of the Church in the area of democracy.[12]

There was a host of questions to explore under both headings. What could be done to maximize the benefits of globalization while minimizing the dislocations and losses that are its inevitable accompaniments? How could it be assured that the poorest individuals and nations would have the basic conditions they need in order to be agents of their own development? What are the conditions necessary to sustain a democratic republic? How can those conditions be fostered?

Sensing that Malinvaud was becoming discouraged, I did my best to be helpful to him. I had many international contacts through my work in international legal studies and was able to assist him in finding outside experts. In those days, it was easier than one might suppose to persuade well-known academics and public figures to speak at a Vatican conference without honorarium and with only round-trip economy-class airfare. Most of the persons I contacted were excited by the prospect of meeting Pope John Paul II. The fact that guest speakers were lodged in the Casa Santa Marta was also a draw. One never knew what distinguished prelates or famous visitors he or she might meet at breakfast, lunch, or dinner. Many of our speakers elected to remain with us for two or three days.

Malinvaud, I believe, came to rely on me as someone who could get things done as well as to prepare a well-documented paper for each meeting. In 2002, he asked me to take charge of the third project that had been envisioned when the academy was founded: intergenerational solidarity. The assignment dovetailed nicely with my academic research on the changes in behavior and ideas that were transforming family relations everywhere in the late twentieth century. The time was overdue for Catholic social thought to take account of developments that were having a powerful effect on the nurture and education of children as well as the family's role as a support institution for its dependent members. The transformation of family life was affecting all the structures of civil society—neighborhoods, schools, parishes, and so on. In a vicious cycle, the mediating institutions of civil society could no longer count on assistance from families and thus were less able to serve as resources for families under stress. Governmental interventions often aggravated the very situations they were meant to help. Complicating the situation was the fact that many of the developments that weakened family ties were closely connected to goods and freedoms that are prized by modern men and women.

In organizing the 2004 plenary meeting, "Intergenerational Solidarity, Welfare, and Human Ecology," I was fortunate to collaborate with a capable Italian sociologist, Pierpaolo Donati. Our aim was to move beyond standard debates over the "welfare crisis," and to focus on the deeper underlying crisis of meanings and values. We wanted to explore how changes in family behavior were fueling, and being fueled by, changes in ideas about dependency, the human person, and family life—and to study the implications of these changes for the world's experiments in self-government, for the health of economies, for human rights, and for the future of our social and natural environments. We asked our guest experts, who included Francis Fukuyama and Jacques Vallin (head of the French National Institute for Demographic Studies), to treat these developments as an "ecological crisis" where social environments, like natural environments, were at risk. We asked them to think about what might be done to foster social conditions more favorable to human flourishing. What could law and policy do to help revitalize families and other fragile seedbeds of character and competence upon which political freedom and economic vitality depend? It seemed clear to us that any family policy that focuses on families alone without attending to their surrounding institutions is doomed to failure. Then, as now, social scientists did not know very much about how to encourage, or even to avoid damage to, the social systems that both undergird and buffer the market and the state.

The report we produced after that meeting drew attention to several emerging issues involving care for the frail elderly that were being overlooked by policy makers.[13] I was pleased that it was unanimously approved by the academicians, and that they favored devoting a second annual meeting to the topic, this time focusing on the effects of demographic trends on children and child-raising families.

In an effort to fulfill the pope's desire for the academy's findings to be communicated to the international social science community, I brought the report to the attention of the U.S. president's Council on Bioethics, of which I was a member. The council then conducted its own study of the ethical dilemmas facing an aging society and published a report titled *Taking Care: Ethical Caregiving in Our Aging Society.* In the introduction, Chairman Leon Kass wrote these words, which could have been penned by John Paul II himself:

Any approach our society takes must attend to the ethical and humanistic dimensions of our situation, not only the economic and institutional ones. For we will be judged as a people by our willingness to stand by one another, even as the flame of life flickers and fades in those who have brought us here and to whom we owe so much.[14]

In 2004, at the end of Edmond Malinvaud's second five-year term, the pope asked me to take over as president of the academy. I was not delighted about the assignment. I had always declined to be considered for administrative positions in the university world, and I regarded many of the challenges Malinvaud had gallantly faced as intractable because of the structure of the academy. But how could I say no to the pope, whose vision and hopes I shared?

My first act was to call Malinvaud to discuss the transition and to get his general advice. It was then that I learned that the chancellor had not bothered to notify the president that his term would not be renewed or to thank him for his service. Nevertheless, Malinvaud graciously shared his perceptions, including his sense that the chancellor, an Argentinian bishop with no credentials in economics, law, sociology, or political science, was using his office in the academy's headquarters as the base for a little fiefdom of his own.

As it happened, the 2004 plenary meeting was our last with John Paul II. Over the years, the high point of these meetings had always been the audience with the pope, where he personally greeted each academician, any family members who accompanied them, and each visiting speaker. But his health was failing rapidly, his speech was hard to understand, and he often seemed to be in pain. Parkinson's disease had frozen his expressive face.

It was hard to keep back tears as I delivered my presidential address to him and then took my place at his side to introduce each participant. He leaned over, took my hands, and said something to me, but his words were so slurred that I had to ask him to say it again. Very slowly, he repeated, "How's the family?"

The last meeting with Pope John Paul II

PART II

The Court of Benedict XVI

So much was his old-fashioned virtue out of the present mode, among the depraved customs which time and luxury had introduced, that it appeared, indeed, remarkable and wonderful, but was too great and too good to suit the present exigencies, being so out of all proportion to the times.

—PLUTARCH,
on Cato the Younger in *The Life of Phocion*

CHAPTER FIVE

"How Would You Like to Be the U.S. Ambassador to the Holy See?"

✣

"I'd like to be an ambassadure," said Mr. Hennessy.
"An' why?" said Mr. Dooley.
"It mus' be a gran' job," said Mr. Hennessy.
"'Tis an aisy job," said Mr. Dooley, "an' 'tis a gran'
job if ye care f'r it."

—FINLEY PETER DUNNE,
Dissertations by Mr. Dooley

In April 2005, I made the sad voyage to Rome to attend the funeral of the man who had deeply affected the lives of so many, including mine. At the end of the ceremony, a gust of wind blew shut the book of the Gospels that had lain open on top of Pope John Paul II's coffin, and I felt as though a chapter in my life had been closed as well.

Where the Pontifical Academy of Social Sciences was concerned, I was hopeful that newly elected Pope Benedict, with his scholarly background, would take a special interest in our work. When I learned that his first official visit to a Vatican department would be to the academy headquarters, I took that as a sign that he might even wish to be personally involved in some of our activities. I prepared my formal welcoming remarks with that idea in mind, relating the predominance of relativistic attitudes in the social sciences to

Welcoming Pope Benedict on his first official visit to the
Pontifical Academy

his recent warning about the "dictatorship of relativism."
Little did I realize that next to the challenges facing the new
pope, the affairs of the academy were pretty small potatoes.

I met Pope Benedict at the entrance to the academy, and as
we walked to the meeting, I asked whether he had any suggestions for studies that might be useful to the Church. He
answered that he would be very pleased if we continued along
the lines that we thought best. That was not what I was hoping to hear, but I soon came to understand that this little corner of the Vatican City State was among the least of his worries.

That year's program on personhood, coordinated by Edmond Malinvaud, who remained an active member, was so
well organized and so fruitful that I began to have hope that
the academy was finally coalescing into a group that could
produce valuable studies. Ever the can-do, if naïve, Ameri-

can, I embarked on a four-part plan to help the process along. The first and most important step was to have a private conversation with each member about his or her hopes for the academy ("if you could change one thing . . ."), and about what he or she would like to contribute. Second, I made strenuous efforts to locate highly qualified candidates for membership, searching for leading scholars who would commit to being actively involved. Third, I began looking for ways to ensure that ideas generated in the academy would get more attention in Vatican circles and in the international academic world. And fourth, I solicited suggestions for topics from members of the curia whom I had come to know.

That last initiative led to a fruitful suggestion from Cardinal Jean-Louis Tauran, who had become a good friend after being my contact person in Beijing. He proposed that the academy explore how Catholic social doctrine's principle of subsidiarity might work in a globalized context. Subsidiarity is a complex but important idea. The simplest way to understand it is that problems should be solved as locally as possible, which means, for example, a national government shouldn't address problems that a regional government can solve, nor a regional government interfere with matters that a municipal government can handle, and so on. In the international arena, subsidiarity is related to principles of freedom, sovereignty, democratic accountability, and federalism. It requires that, wherever possible, decisions ought to be made at the level closest to the persons affected by them—starting with their primary communities—and that larger, more general and distant communities should intervene only to help the primary ones, not to replace them. In a globalizing world, where people are often disconnected from local communities, or where a local problem is inseparable from a global problem—like many environmental challenges—subsidiarity becomes even more complex.

It would be useful, Cardinal Tauran said, if "the theme of subsidiarity were developed, linking it to the principle of solidarity and to international governance, in relation also to the problems of multilateralism and to the far-ranging questions of development/poverty/responsibility (e.g., Millennium Development Goals) and security/disarmament/use of force/humanitarian intervention."

That suggestion was especially welcome to me. Catholic international relations theory was badly in need of *aggiornamento*. In particular, few experts on subsidiarity in Catholic social thought had discussed it in the context of international relations.

Catholic discussions of the subsidiarity concept had been concerned mainly with the relationship between the nation-state and the intermediate institutions of civil society. What needed study was how to apply the doctrine in the globalized twenty-first-century world, where many nations had yielded some of their sovereignty to supranational entities like the European Union, where national sovereignty was eroded in some respects by economic forces, and where increasing numbers of problems could be handled only by cooperation at the international level. For once, academy members collaborated well, producing two volumes of excellent material.

The academicians had hoped that their essays identifying internal tensions in Catholic international relations theory would lead to fruitful discussions with members of the curia on how to apply the doctrine of subsidiarity to concrete, real-world problems. The Holy See's approach to poverty and development, for example, emphasized the need to bring the poorest peoples into the circle of productivity and exchange in keeping with the UN's Millennium Development Goals, but not much thought had been given to how the harmful effects of globalization on the freedom and integrity of local cultures could be minimized.

The academicians also recommended more careful attention to how the Holy See's strong support of international institutions could be related to the subsidiarity principle, which emphasizes respect for the integrity of nation-states and other bodies of a lower order.

We shared our volumes with the Pontifical Council for Justice and Peace and with the Secretary for Relations with States who had succeeded Cardinal Tauran in that position, but disappointingly, we received no response.

We did succeed, however, in getting wider attention for the academy's work. Thanks to a generous donor, I secured the funds to bring a respected Canadian Catholic journalist, Father Raymond de Souza, to our meetings as liaison with the press during our plenaries. Then I prevailed on my slight acquaintance with some high-profile individuals like Henry Kissinger, Cherie Blair, and Wikipedia cofounder Jimmy Wales to invite them to speak at our plenaries and to be available for press conferences. All three were big hits with the press and very generous with their time. A few members grumbled about the invitations to Kissinger and Blair on political grounds, but both speakers made valuable contributions, and it seemed to me that those invitations were fully in keeping with the practice recommended by Pope John Paul II to search for fragments of truth wherever they may be found.

Kissinger's speech was noteworthy for his musings on the

life of a policy maker as distinct from that of a scholar. "As a professor," he said, "I could choose my subjects, and I could work on them for as long as I chose. As a policy maker, I was always pressed for time. . . . As a professor, I was responsible for coming up with the best answer I could divine. As a policy maker, I was also responsible for the worst that could happen. As a professor, the risk was that the important would drive out the urgent. As a policy maker, the risk was that the urgent would drive out the important."

He agreed, he said, with what John Paul II had once said to him, that the role of the Church was to stand for truth and that "truth cannot be modified according to the contingencies of the moment." But, said Kissinger, the policy maker, living in the world of the contingent, "must deal with answers that hopefully are on the road to truth" with the terrible knowledge that "the attempt to achieve the ultimate in a finite period of time can produce extraordinary disasters." He concluded, ruefully, "It may take some divine guidance and not just insight to solve the problem."

In Kissinger's case, I was concerned that the rather austere accommodations at the Casa Santa Marta might not be to his taste, so I offered to make reservations for him at a nearby hotel. But he insisted that he wanted to have the experience of staying in the Vatican. The Casa Santa Marta, though sometimes described by reporters who have never seen it as luxurious, is more like a dorm or a monastery than a hotel. Each chamber is equipped with a bed, a dresser, a desk, bookshelves, an armchair, a straight-backed chair, and, in recent years, a television. Simple meals (whatever is being served that day, take it or leave it) are served at set times in a common dining room.

That, it seems, was not quite what Dr. Kissinger expected. When I came to pick him up after his first night in the Casa for a tour of the Vatican Museums, he mentioned his surprise that there was no room service. At a party the following year, he introduced me as the person who had kept him prisoner in the Vatican.

One Saturday morning in July 2007, the phone rang. When I answered, I did not expect to hear the voice of Karl Rove, President George W. Bush's deputy chief of staff, whom I had met only briefly while visiting the White House to discuss religious freedom and bioethics issues.

"How would you like to be the U.S. Ambassador to the Holy See?" he asked. He explained that a vacancy had occurred because Ambassador Francis Rooney wished to return to private life.

The call came just as I was in the midst of writing a book about the ambivalence of Plato, Tocqueville, Max Weber, and others who were torn between scholarship and public life. A prudent response surely would have been "That sounds interesting. I'd like to think about it" or "Tell me more about the position." But I did not hesitate a second before saying, "Yes, I'd like that very much!" In truth, there wasn't much to ponder since I knew Edward would be as enthusiastic as I was, and I was sure that my dean, Elena Kagan, would be pleased too. Harvard Law School prided itself on a tradition of public service, and since President Bush would be leaving office in January 2009, the assignment would take me away from home and the school for only a little more than a year.

On the day my nomination was publicly announced, I sat down with a number of colleagues in the law school's faculty lunchroom. When I mentioned that I might be taking a leave to serve as Ambassador to the Holy See, Louis Loss, the father of modern securities law, misheard me. "You're going to the SEC?" he asked excitedly. Another colleague corrected him, "No, she's going to the Vatican."

Strictly speaking, the second colleague was mistaken too. But the terms Vatican and Holy See are so regularly used interchangeably that many people assume they are synonyms. It's easier to say, "the Vatican," as I often do, than to explain the unique nature of the Holy See. But the distinction is important where international relations are concerned.

It is the Holy See, not the Vatican, that is a sovereign entity with diplomatic relations with some 183 states, as well as permanent observer status at the United Nations and other international bodies. It has its headquarters in Vatican City, an independent city-state that was created by treaty between the Holy See and Italy in 1929 and made subject to the sovereign authority of the Holy See. The dual nature of the Holy See as both a sovereign entity and the universal government of the Roman Catholic Church is a hard concept to grasp, even for international lawyers, since an internationally recognized sovereign entity that is not confined to a particular geographical territory does not fit into any of the usual categories.

As the table talk continued, a young professor asked, "Why does the United States have diplomatic relations with a church?" That question is so common that State Department staffers told me to expect it from senators at my confirmation hearing. The answer requires a bit of history.

Informal contacts between the United States and the Papal States were established almost as soon as our nation became a sovereign state.[1] In 1788, President George Washington commissioned Benjamin Franklin to inform Pope Pius VI that, contrary to the practice in many European countries, the pope would not need to request permission from the United States before appointing bishops here.[2] At the height of the Civil War, and in the waning days of the Papal States, President Abraham Lincoln sent an official legate to the court of Pope Pius IX. Addressing the pope as "Great and Good Friend," Lincoln explained that his aim in sending a representative was to "cultivate and strengthen the friendship and good correspondence between us."[3] Such contacts were infrequent, however, until 1940, when President Franklin Roosevelt appointed industrialist and diplomat Myron Taylor as a special envoy to Pope Pius XII to help the United States keep abreast of European events. When World War II ended, President Harry Truman announced his intention to formalize this relationship, which had proved useful to his predecessor. He soon found, however, that he had seriously underestimated the political opposition to such a move.

One illustration will suffice. Eleanor Roosevelt, for all her open-mindedness on many subjects, had one bias that she was apparently unable to overcome. Her Jewish friend and adviser Joseph Lash wrote in his memoir that he was always "struck by her hostility to the Catholic Church."[4] Lash speculated, "Somewhere deep in her subconscious was an anti-Catholicism which was a part of her Protestant heritage." When Mrs. Roosevelt learned that President Truman was planning to exchange ambassadors with the Holy See, she added her influential voice to the torrent of protest he was receiving:

I have not written you anything before but I am afraid I must now break my silence about the appointment of an ambassador to the Vatican.... I feel that perhaps I should tell you it seems to me since we are a Protestant country, we should heed the very evident feeling so many Protestants have against having an ambassador at the Vatican.... For the purpose of the US, I have always felt that a special representative gave all the advantages and avoided the pitfalls which the appointment of an ambassador or minister brings about,... The recognition of any church as a temporal power puts that church in a different position from any of the other churches and while we are now only hearing from the Protestant groups, the Moslems may one day wake up to this and make an equal howl.[5]

Eleanor Roosevelt, then the most admired woman in the United States, was only one of many persons who sent objections to the president. There was so much pressure, including from Truman's own Protestant minister, that he backed down.

The question of formalizing the relationship did not arise again until 1984. By that time, President Ronald Reagan and Pope John Paul II were both convinced that the seemingly indestructible Soviet Empire not only could fall, but would. Believing that the Polish pope would be an important ally in that cause, Reagan determined to establish full diplomatic relations with the Holy See, with the strong support of Senator Richard Lugar, a Methodist. Addressing critics, Lugar said, "The Vatican is a sensitive focus of international relations. It is also a sovereign state, and with John Paul's courage and character, a powerful force for decency in the world."[6] In many respects, he added, "the Vatican is a far more significant and wide-ranging actor than many of the other governments with which we maintain formal relations."[7]

Public opinion polls showed approval for the idea from Protestants and Catholics alike, but there was strong opposition from militant secularists and some Protestant leaders when President Reagan announced that he was appointing a friend of his, businessman William Wilson, as the first U.S. ambassador to the Holy See. Opponents filed suit, challenging the constitutionality of sending an ambassador to "a church," but the dismissal of their complaint was affirmed by a federal appeals court, holding that "questions of diplomatic relations are committed by the Constitution to final decision by the Executive Branch and thus present non-justiciable political questions."[8]

Today, when people, like my young colleague, ask why the United States has diplomatic relations with "a church," I imagine that what many of them really want to know is what *value* the United States gets from exchanging ambassadors with an entity as peculiar as the Holy See. The short answer is that the global reach and impact of the Holy See can affect U.S. interests and image in nearly every corner of the world. After the formal relationship had been in place for several years, former Secretary of State Colin Powell described it as a "unique partnership" in which two entities with worldwide concerns shared a broad range of values and ideals.[9]

As a practical matter, the Holy See has long been recognized by the United States and other countries as a valuable listening post. One of the main tasks of diplomatic envoys is to gather and report on useful information, and the Holy See, with a presence in nearly every corner of the globe, often has access to types of information that are difficult for other entities to obtain. An 1865 report from President Lincoln's legate shows that the papal court was appreciated for that reason even then. "Rome," he wrote, "is a great center of news. Everything going on, all over the world, is known there." But to get at that information, he explained, American representatives needed to conduct themselves as continental diplomats did. "European diplomacy is carried on by dinners and parties—you gather information in this way to be obtained in no other manner."[10]

One could easily imagine a similar letter being written today, right down to its concluding paragraph, where the author warns that Russia "needs watching and she has her spies in every country and knows well what is going on. I have no doubt that she has spies in the State Department possibly in men who profess to hate her. The Russians are considered the greatest intriguers in Europe controlling presses and shaping public opinion."

Today, even more than in the nineteenth century, Vatican officials have a constant supply of grassroots information from Catholic health care facilities, schools, and relief organizations all over the world, plus a global network of parishes, priests, dioceses, bishops, male and female religious communities, and missionaries. Thanks to these varied sources, the Holy See is well positioned to know what is actually going on in the capillaries of societies where the United States has little or no presence. In a backhanded tribute, Henry Kissinger once quipped that the Holy See collects a great deal of intelligence from all over the world but doesn't know how to use it.

Not long after Karl Rove's phone call I discovered how

complicated and time-consuming it can be to enter federal employment. All through the summer of 2007, there were endless forms to fill out—detailed financial disclosures, names of all the organizations I belonged to, addresses of every place I had ever lived, plus all the foreign countries to which I had traveled and the dates of every trip. (Fortunately I had saved my old passports and calendars.) I was extensively interviewed by a pleasant agent who asked me to give him contact information for ten persons, not relatives, who knew me well. Naturally, I supplied the names of people who, I hoped, would say nice things about me. What happens next, I discovered, is that each of these persons is then interviewed and asked for the names of more persons, and so it goes until the investigators are satisfied that they have a fairly full picture of the candidate.

Since the president's choice could not be announced until all these preliminaries had been completed, I began to receive calls from colleagues, old friends, and former co-workers, some of whom I hadn't seen for years. Dean Kagan was the first to ask, "Why is a government agent asking me all these questions about you?"

That experience prompted me, when giving talks to law students, to make a point of advising them to keep in mind that they someday might need a security clearance. Even if they don't expect to be considered for a government position, they should be aware that many private employers perform extensive searches before hiring. "When your thoughts turn to Facebook," I say, "open your casebook."

Once my security clearance was approved, the White House announced my nomination and I began to prepare for my confirmation hearing before the Senate Foreign Affairs

Committee, then chaired by Senator Joseph Biden. I was touched that my pro-choice colleague Larry Tribe was one of the first to offer me congratulations and support: "Just in case you or the people in the administration who are handling the confirmation want a liberal Jewish university professor from an eastern institution of higher learning who is in his sixties and who disagrees with you strongly about *Roe v. Wade* but is confident you'll make the ideal ambassador and is wildly in favor of your confirmation, I suspect I know just the guy, and I can say without fear of contradiction that he'd be absolutely delighted to testify for you."

Preparation for confirmation involved many trips to Washington for briefings at the State Department, consultations at the White House, and courtesy calls to various senators. Everything seemed to be proceeding smoothly until a State Department official called to inform me that Senator Biden's office was opposing my confirmation on the ground that I had failed to register as a foreign agent under the Foreign Agents Registration Act—a felony punishable by fine or up to five years' imprisonment.

Biden's staff made that very serious charge because they saw on the forms I submitted that I had served the Holy See in various capacities over the years. What they didn't do, apparently, was read the act, which contains a specific exemption for "activities in furtherance of bona fide religious, scholastic, academic, or scientific pursuits." The State Department's lawyers quickly prepared and sent Biden a memo showing that my services for the Holy See were not covered by the statute. Nevertheless, his office persisted in holding up the process.

By that time, it was well into November and time was running out. The Senate would soon recess for the Christmas holidays, and if I was not confirmed before that, it would hardly be worthwhile to pursue Senate approval for a position that would then last for less than a year. There had been no ambassadorial nominee hearings since October 17, and rumors were circulating that the Democratic majority in the Senate was not disposed to hold any more hearings on political appointees at this late stage in the Bush administration. Some newspapers were reporting that my nomination was "dead in the water."

Fate—well, actually Realpolitik—intervened. A few months before Karl Rove had called me about the ambassadorship, the family of Eunice Kennedy Shriver had asked me to officiate at a gala celebration in her honor, to be held on November 16 at the Kennedy Library in Boston. The plan for the evening was that the Shriver children would sit on a stage with an interlocutor who would introduce the program and ask the children questions that were designed to bring out their favorite memories of their mother and to highlight her most important achievements. The plan had been submitted to Eunice for her approval, with the suggestion that Tim Russert, longtime moderator of NBC TV's *Meet the Press,* should lead the discussion. But Eunice—ever her own woman—had said, "No, I want Mary Ann Glendon to do it."

I gladly accepted the invitation. Eunice was a friend and a truly great American woman whose tireless activities on behalf of the intellectually disabled had enlarged the sense of the human family to which we all belong. As the doting grandmother of a young man with Down syndrome, I had unbounded admiration for Eunice's pioneering work in founding the Special Olympics. I first met her in the 1970s when Larry Tribe put us in touch after she had asked him, "Aren't there any law professors who are pro-life?" She and I quickly found that we shared the understanding that "pro-life" included being pro-woman and pro-poor. She told me more than once that one of her greatest sorrows was that she had not been able to convince her brothers and sisters that the Democratic Party was the natural home for policies protecting the most vulnerable of human beings.

On the night of November 16, Eunice appeared alarmingly frail, a wraith in a silver dress spangled with rose and green sequins. Only two days later she collapsed and was hospitalized, an increasingly frequent experience for her. But she rose to the occasion that evening when she spoke to the hundreds of well-wishers who had gathered at the library. She chose to devote most of her remarks to the influence that her mentally impaired sister, Rosemary, had had on the Kennedy family. It was witnessing the "unbearable rejection" that Rosemary had suffered, she said, that had determined her to make the world a better place for people with intellectual disabilities.

My public conversation with the Shriver children elicited fond and funny memories from Bobby, Maria, Mark, and Anthony (Timothy was unable to attend). The program was followed by a dinner, during which I had the opportunity to tell Senator Ted Kennedy about the problems I was having with the staff of his friend Senator Biden. I had met Ted only once before, at a small dinner organized by my colleague Michael Sandel for the senator, Cornel West, and me, but he said he remembered that evening well and listened while I pointed out that it would be important for the United States to have an ambassador in place in order to prepare properly for Pope Benedict's forthcoming April visit to the United States.

Emceeing Eunice Kennedy's eightieth birthday celebration

"Your friend Joe Biden is blocking my confirmation hearing."

It cannot be a coincidence that a few days later I was notified to go to Washington for a hearing before the Senate Foreign Relations Committee on my confirmation. The hearing was brief. There were only two nominees before the committee: Charles W. Larson Jr., of Iowa, who had been nominated to be ambassador to Latvia, and me. Presiding in lieu of Senator Biden was Senator Robert Casey Jr., whose late father, Governor Bob Casey, and I had become friends as members of the Catholic Common Ground Initiative.

I briefly described the experiences in international settings that would aid me in promoting America's interests abroad. Since most of my legal work, academic writing, and pro bono activity had been concentrated in areas where the United States and the Holy See had common concerns, I told the committee that I expected to be vigorously involved in the collaboration that had already been established on a range of issues, including human rights, religious freedom, trafficking in persons, development, and the fight against hunger, disease, and poverty. Anticipating questions about whether my various services to the Holy See would give rise to any conflicts of interest, I made clear that I was looking forward to advocating for my country and that I believed the knowledge and understanding of the Holy See I had acquired would help me to serve the United States well. No questions were asked, and I was unanimously confirmed by the Senate later that day.

There were many times during the confirmation process when it was hard to avoid ironic reflection about Vatican II's exhortation to the laity to take up "the noble art of politics."

Nothing I had seen in Washington in the preceding months seemed very noble, nor did I have illusions about politics within the Holy See, but I was looking forward to meeting its diplomats, whose mandate was to serve as moral witnesses while dealing with everyday political realities.

CHAPTER SIX

From Harvard to Embassy Vatican

✢

Forget about privacy.

—STATE DEPARTMENT OFFICIAL to new ambassadors

As 2007 drew to a close, I was in a whirlwind of preparations for assuming my duties as the eighth American to serve as U.S. Ambassador to the Holy See. Since the assignment would last only a little more than a year, Edward and I had decided that he would remain at home in Chestnut Hill to be doted on by our Boston-based daughters, Sarah and Katie. Thanks to direct flights between Rome and Boston, we would be able to get together frequently. Before my departure, however, there were a number of mandatory briefings and orientation programs in Washington.

Two of the obligatory programs I attended that week were "Diversity Awareness" and "Security Overseas." In the first, a government employee admonished future ambassadors never, ever to stereotype. In the second, a hardened ex-CIA agent told us always, always to profile because doing so can save your life. I wondered if they went out for a drink together afterward. Probably not.

After one of these sessions, a State Department official mentioned something that had not crossed my mind. "Forget about privacy," he said. He told me that once I set foot on the soil of Italy, I would never be alone. I would be guarded day and night whether in my residence or at the embassy. If I wanted to take a walk, or go somewhere by train, I would be accompanied. If I wanted to travel by car, I would be taken in an armored vehicle and accompanied by police cars. If I wanted to go to a restaurant, my escorts would be there too, keeping me in sight. As the person responsible for all the employees in my embassy, I would be on duty seven days a week, twenty-four hours a day, and could expect to be wakened at odd hours for emergencies. "Buy a bathrobe," he said. As soon as I got home, I bought two bathrobes, just in case.

As part of my preparation, I also read Pope Benedict's traditional New Year's address to the ambassadors to the Holy See. I was excited to see that he emphasized religious freedom and that he mentioned the upcoming sixtieth anniversary of the 1948 Universal Declaration of Human Rights. Both of those topics already figured in my plans for the next few months. Ever since the preceding July, I had known that I would have to hit the ground running in order to make the best use of the year ahead. The fact that the sixtieth anniversary of the UDHR coincided with the twenty-fifth anniversary of formal diplomatic relations between the United States and the Holy See had given me the idea to organize a series of international conferences around themes of common interest to both entities. Now, after reading the Holy Father's speech, I was confident that I had been on the right track when I chose religious liberty as the theme for the grand finale conference commemorating the anniversary of diplomatic relations.

After the briefings at the State Department were finished, there was just one more step before heading to Rome. Ordinarily, an ambassador takes his or her oath of office in Washington. But since Dean Kagan, who had been wonderfully supportive throughout the process, was eager to give me a send-off party, I decided to be sworn in at the law school. My friend Michael Boudin, then Chief Judge of the United States Court of Appeals for the First Circuit, administered the oath, and Elena, never one to do things halfway, provided a champagne reception for my family members, friends, and colleagues. A few hours later, I took the overnight flight to Rome.

Even though I had been well briefed on security concerns, I was not quite prepared for the reality of twenty-four-hour police protection. On that first day, and every day thereafter when I traveled by car, the embassy vehicle in which I sat was preceded and followed by a Roman police car. In Rome, only the ambassadors of the United States, Israel, and Turkey were so heavily guarded—the United States and Israel because of constant threats, and Turkey because a Turkish envoy had been assassinated there a few years previously.

As a law professor, I had enjoyed about as much freedom as any working person has. Now I realized how different things were going to be. No more wandering around Rome on foot, savoring the sounds, smells, and sights. No more spur-of-the-moment visits to a museum, shop, or trattoria, since police escorts had to be notified in advance of any outing.

The most memorable event of my first days in Rome was the formal presentation of my credentials to Pope Benedict XVI. Though I had met the Holy Father on previous occasions when he visited the Pontifical Academy of Social Sciences, I had tended to think of him as a fellow academic who had been catapulted into the type of work that most academics most dislike—administration. In the simple cassock he wore on visits to the academy, the pope had indeed seemed like one of us.

The solemn credentials ceremony, however, introduced me to Benedict XVI as the successor of Peter and the Holy See's head of state. The meeting with him in the Apostolic Palace gave me some sense of the awesome responsibilities this scholarly priest had undertaken. Only much later, when I served on Pope Francis's commission to investigate the Vatican Bank, did I realize what a terrible weight had been placed on those slender shoulders.

On the morning of the credentials ceremony, I and my daughters, Elizabeth, Sarah, and Katherine, and granddaughters, Claire and Giulia, donned our long black dresses and helped each other with our lace mantillas. Precisely at 10:30 A.M., two gentlemen of the papal court in white tie and tails arrived to escort us for the duration. As our motorcade wound its way from the quiet of the Janiculum to the bustle surrounding the Piazza San Pietro and the entrance to the Vatican, they explained every detail of what to expect.

Once inside the Vatican gates, all was quiet again. We drove past the *governato,* the administrative headquarters of the city-state, and through Italian-style formal gardens (lots of greenery, not much color) to a narrow stone passageway opening into the Courtyard of Saint Damasus outside the Apostolic Palace. There we were met by a detachment of Swiss Guards, who presented arms and ushered us into the wood-paneled elevators that took us to the floor of the papal receiving rooms.

We passed through the Sala Clementina, a large, high-vaulted hall adorned with Renaissance frescoes and gleaming floors of pink, white, green, and yellow marble. This room was familiar to me since the members of the Pontifical Academy of Social Sciences had often been received there. Gradually the rooms got smaller until we came to a more intimate reception area outside the papal apartments. There my daughters and granddaughters were left to contemplate paintings by Raphael and Fra Bartolomeo, while the American prefect of the papal household, Archbishop (now Cardinal) James Harvey, accompanied me to the pope's private library. There in the doorway, Pope Benedict in red and gold regalia received my credentials and we exchanged prepared formal remarks.

With hindsight, the pope's remarks were a preview of the themes he would stress during his visit to the United States. He said he was looking forward to the visit, and he described the United States as "a nation that values the role of religious belief in ensuring a vibrant and ethically sound democratic order" and as an example of how diversity can be reconciled

Presentation of credentials to Pope Benedict XVI

with commitment to the common good.[11] As in his January talk to the diplomatic corps, he referenced the sixtieth anniversary of the Universal Declaration of Human Rights and spoke of religious freedom. The sentiments he expressed about the role of religion in public life mirrored the views of President Bush on that subject:

> The American people's historic appreciation of the role of religion in shaping public discourse and in shedding light on the inherent moral dimension of social issues—a role at times contested in the name of a straitened understanding of political life and public discourse—is reflected in the efforts of so many of your fellow-citizens and government leaders to ensure legal protection for God's gift of life from conception to natural death, and the safeguarding of the institution of marriage, acknowledged as a stable union between a man and a woman, and that of the family.

I was touched that he mentioned my previous service in the Vatican, saying that he was "confident that the knowledge and experience born of your distinguished association with the work of the Holy See will prove beneficial in the fulfillment of your duties and enrich the activity of the diplomatic community to which you now belong."[12]

In my formal reply, I transmitted the greetings of President Bush and pledged continuation of our efforts toward the many goals we shared with the Holy See, especially forging an international consensus against terrorism and the misuse of religion as a pretext for violence, and seeking creative ways to reduce hunger, disease, and poverty worldwide.[13]

With formalities completed, the library door closed and we sat down for a private talk, where we spoke, he somewhat ruefully, I thought, about scholarship as a vocation and politics as a duty. Afterward, the pope greeted my daughters and granddaughters, and I proceeded to the Secretariat of State for a private talk with the secretary, Cardinal Tarcisio Bertone, whom Benedict had appointed to succeed John Paul II's secretary, longtime diplomat Cardinal Angelo Sodano.

It was my first meeting with the cardinal, who had been secretary of the Congregation for the Doctrine of the Faith while Cardinal Ratzinger was prefect, and I must admit I left without having gained a sense of the real person in the chair opposite mine. Like many other Catholics, I had been somewhat surprised when Pope Benedict chose his former associate, rather than a more experienced administrator or diplomat, to be in charge of all the political and diplomatic functions of the Holy See. It was understandable that the pope was comfortable working with an old and trusted colleague, but with hindsight it was an early sign that Benedict XVI, like John Paul II, was not going to be deeply involved in administration.

We spoke briefly and in a general way about relations between the United States and the Holy See. By that time Vatican officials had no disposition to revisit the controversy over the United States's military action in Iraq. Though the Holy See had vigorously opposed that intervention, they now regarded the idea of a precipitate withdrawal as posing great danger for Christians and other religious minorities. Having chaired the subcommittee on Iraq for the Committee on International Justice and Peace of the U.S. Conference of Catholic Bishops in 2002, I was well aware of how contentious that issue could be, even among Catholic prelates. I was relieved that discussions relating to Iraq during my tenure as ambassador could focus on our common concern for the establishment of stability, peace, and protection of minorities in the region.

After the meetings with Pope Benedict and Cardinal Bertone, I rejoined my family and the papal gentlemen for a part of the credential ceremony that is reserved for Catholic ambassadors, a solemn visit to the Basilica of Saint Peter. As my daughter Elizabeth described it for the Zenit news agency:

> Four Swiss Guards took their places around the new Ambassador. With their halberds raised, they formed a protective curtain around her. The stately procession made its way down the stairs to the colorful halls of the Sala Regia and Sala Ducale, until we reached the Royal Stairs, the dramatic descent from the Sistine Chapel to Saint Peter's Basilica and Square. Turning into the bronze portals, we saw the immense nave of St. Peter's stretched out before us; the ambassador's cortege was tracing the same route as the papal procession for Mass.[14]

When we entered the basilica, I saw that almost the entire nave had been cordoned off for the purpose of permitting me to pray quietly at three holy places. With crowds of tourists watching this unusual scene from behind the ropes, and with my knees beginning to tremble, I was escorted to a red velvet kneeler before the Chapel of the Blessed Sacrament to spend a few moments with the exposed Eucharist. I was then taken to the altar of the Gregorian Chapel, where the image of the Madonna of Perpetual Succor is displayed, and finally to the heart of the basilica, where I knelt at the Altar of the Confession over the tomb of Saint Peter and offered prayers for my country and for Peter's successor.

CHAPTER SEVEN

Pope Benedict and the President Who "Spoke Catholic"

✤

Your Holiness, when people ask me why I came out here to meet you today, I tell them it's because you're the greatest spiritual leader in the whole world.

—PRESIDENT GEORGE W. BUSH
to Pope Benedict XVI at Andrews Air Force Base

Because the Holy See is a unique sovereignty, the job of the men and women who are posted to Embassy Vatican (as the State Department calls it) is like no other assignment in the U.S. Foreign Service. As in other embassies, much of the day-to-day work involves the age-old business of gathering information and writing reports after endless meetings, receptions, lunches, and dinners. But in Embassy Vatican there are no commercial or military affairs to handle and no visas to issue. Looming large on the agenda of that unusual diplomatic mission is what is known as public diplomacy—activities aimed at advancing the interests, values, and image of the United States. In the early weeks of 2008, information gathering and public diplomacy occupied most of our time as we assisted in preparations for Pope Benedict's April visit to the White House.

Spring arrives early in Rome. By mid-February, Dante the gardener was already removing the pansies (which he called "winter flowers") and tending to the rosebushes around the embassy building, which were already starting to bloom. The building itself was an unimposing structure whose best feature was its location in the historic area between the Aventine and Palatine Hills close to the Circus Maximus, the scene of ancient Roman chariot races and entertainments. Built in 1953 as a private residence, it later housed a Soviet embassy, and in 1994 was acquired by the U.S. government. In 2015, the Obama administration would relocate the embassy to the compound occupied by the U.S. embassy to Italy, a move that made sense from the point of view of costs and security. Many in the Holy See, however, viewed it as a sign that the new administration had little interest in the bilateral relationship.

It was my good fortune that the Foreign Service officers with whom I worked in the early months were consummate professionals and dedicated public servants. On the day of my arrival, we gathered in the living room of Villa Richardson (the ambassadorial residence on the Janiculum Hill), and I made clear that it was my desire to learn as much as I could from them as quickly as possible, given the brevity of my assignment. I described my plans for a series of five public events dedicated to common concerns of the United States and the Holy See and was gratified that they seemed enthusiastic.

In the weeks leading up to the pope's visit to the United States, the White House staff pressed us for all the information and suggestions we could supply relating to topics and objectives for the meetings that would take place between President Bush and Pope Benedict, as well as between Secretary of State Condoleezza Rice and Cardinal Secretary of State Bertone.

The relationship between the two heads of state had already gotten off to a good start when President Bush visited the Vatican the preceding June. Those discussions had been aided by their common outlook on a wide range of social and cultural issues and by the fact that the pope was aware of President Bush's deep Christian faith. They had spoken of their shared commitments to strengthening the moral consensus against terrorism; combatting the use of religion as a pretext for terrorism; advancing peace in the Middle East and other troubled regions; addressing the plight of persecuted Christian minorities; promoting interfaith understanding; and strengthening human rights, especially religious freedom, around the world. The earlier disagreement between the United States and the Holy See over Iraq was no longer an obstacle since the pope and Vatican diplomats were now focused on the risk that an abrupt American withdrawal would lead to increased instability and persecution, not only in Iraq but in other parts of the Middle East.

In my memos for U.S. officials and briefings for journalists who would be covering the trip, I built on that background, stressing points that I felt were too often neglected by the press. I hoped that at least some journalists would take note of the fact that the meeting between President Bush and Pope Benedict would be an encounter between the leader of the world's largest donor of humanitarian assistance and the overseer of the world's largest network of hands-on providers of health care, education, and general aid to the poorest people in the poorest parts of the world.[15] I highlighted the facts that President Bush had doubled development assistance to Africa in his first term; that he had stepped up measures for relief of malaria, tuberculosis, and waterborne diseases that take a deadly toll, mainly on children; and that his PEPFAR program (President's Emergency Plan for AIDS Relief) had provided treatment for 1.4 million people living with AIDS in Africa, Asia, and the Caribbean.

To help obtain the best possible press coverage of the encounter, the embassy public affairs officer, Adam Packer, and his assistant, Amy Roth, put together a kit for journalists in an attractive souvenir format. We assumed that many members of the press would be short on background, so we included in each packet information explaining the unique relationship between the United States and the Holy See, a letter from me describing the current state of that relationship, and a signed copy of former Ambassador Jim Nicholson's fine book on the history of the relationship. As requests for interviews poured in, I accepted each one, spurred on by the indefatigable Amy, who was always ready with a pep talk and a cup of strong espresso. In the end, the press coverage exceeded our expectations, in both quantity and quality. *The New York Times* had the pope on its front page for the entire five days of his trip, and the Mass in Yankee Stadium was broadcast on every major American TV station. To my regret, however, there was hardly any mention of the humanitarian concerns shared by the president and the pope.

During Holy Week, which occurred early that year, our frenetic activities came to a halt. For Catholics, the period from Holy Thursday through Good Friday to the evening before Easter Sunday—called the Triduum—is the culmination of the liturgical year. On solemn holy days, the ambassadors to the Holy See attend the liturgies at Saint Peter's Basilica as a body, and they are seated according to the date they presented their credentials. The men wear white tie and

tails; the women are in long black dresses and black mantillas. On one such occasion that year, I was in such a hurry
when I left the residence that I forgot my mantilla. When I
arrived at the basilica, the impeccably attired Egyptian ambassador, a Muslim, kindly handed me her extra black scarf,
saying, "My dear, you must always keep your head covered at
Mass." I will never forget that Easter Triduum, nor any of the
other Masses celebrated by Pope Benedict with his precise
Latin diction, and the age-old liturgies that bind all Catholics, living and dead, into one mystical body.

Although the exact content of the speeches the pope would
give in the United States was closely guarded, I learned in late
March that he would continue to emphasize the dire situation
of Christians in the Middle East, that his UN speech would
reiterate the need for human rights to have a firm philosophical grounding, and that he would address the sex abuse crisis, thus putting to rest speculation about whether he would
tackle that thorny subject. As it turned out, all the major
themes of Pope Benedict's American speeches were prefig-
ured in his January World Day of Peace message and in his
address to me upon receiving my credentials in February.[16]

In early April, Archbishop Pietro Sambi, then the papal
nuncio to the United States, announced that the main purpose
of the pope's visit was pastoral. It would be the visit "of a religious leader, of a friend of humanity and a friend of the United
States who will speak in a spirit of friendship to the citizens of
this country." Pope Benedict followed up with a video message in the same vein, adding that he hoped his presence
would also "be seen as a fraternal gesture towards every ecclesial community, and a sign of friendship for members of other
religious traditions and all men and women of good will."[17]

On April 15, the pope flew to Washington with some sixty journalists and several Holy See officials. En route, he held a press conference in which he said his trip had two main purposes: a visit to the Church in America at a moment when reflection was needed on "how to respond to the great challenges of our time," and a visit to the United Nations at a moment when reflection was needed on the philosophical grounding of the Universal Declaration of Human Rights, to which the nations of the world had committed themselves sixty years earlier.

Sounding a theme that he would elaborate on further in many venues, Pope Benedict told the journalists that he was "fascinated" by the fact that the United States "began with a positive concept of secularism,"[18] an approach to the relation between church and state that is marked by respect for religion and its public role, rather than by hostility to religion. The American founders, he observed, had "intentionally created a secular state" not out of antagonism toward religion—quite the contrary—but out of respect for it. He drew a sharp contrast with the "negative" European form of secularism, noting that the branch of the Enlightenment that was essentially anticlerical and irreligious had had little influence in early America—so little, in fact, that the American system was devised to protect religion and churches from government, not to protect government from religion and churches.

Having flown to Washington a few days earlier, I went out to Andrews Air Force Base to join a small delegation awaiting the pope's arrival. President Bush, who had never before gone to the airport to personally greet a visiting head of state, was in high spirits. "A lot of people," he told us, "asked me why I was going out to meet the pope. It's very simple: He's the greatest spiritual leader in the world." When the pope arrived, the two men sat down for an orange juice, and the president reiterated what he had said earlier: "Your Holiness, when people ask me why I came out here to meet you today, I tell them it's because you're the greatest spiritual leader in the whole world." After a few more pleasantries, the pope was taken to the Apostolic Nunciature to rest before commencing his grueling schedule of nineteen talks in five days. As the president was leaving, he told me, "You'll be sitting between me and McCain at dinner tomorrow night."

The following day, President and Mrs. Bush welcomed the pope to the White House with a colorful ceremony on the South Lawn. The Star-Spangled Banner and the Holy See's gold and white flag waved side by side in the spring breeze while the president told the crowd how happy he was that Pope Benedict had chosen to spend his eighty-first birthday in America. The ten thousand or so guests spontaneously broke into "Happy Birthday." The shy pope beamed, rose, and spread his arms as if to embrace everyone there.

The brief remarks of the president and pope sounded like a duet on the free society with each one singing the other's part. The president said the measure of a free society is how we treat the weakest and most vulnerable among us; the pope echoed Tocqueville and George Washington, saying that the preservation of freedom requires the cultivation of virtue, self-discipline, and a sense of responsibility for the less fortunate. As on the plane, he took the occasion to express his respect for America's "vast pluralistic society" and his appreciation for "a nation that welcomes the role of religion in the public square."[19]

On this occasion, however, the pope's words of praise were accompanied by a note of caution. He warned that religious freedom cannot be taken for granted, and that its erosion could have deleterious effects on the American democratic experiment. "Freedom," he said, "is ever new." Its maintenance "demands the courage to engage in civic life and to bring one's deepest beliefs and values to reasoned public debate. . . . It is a challenge held out to each generation, and must constantly be won over for the cause of good."[20] When the pope concluded, President Bush said, "Thank you, Your Holiness. Awesome speech."

The ceremony ended with a few rousing musical pieces played by a military band. During "The Battle Hymn of the Republic," I noticed Cardinal Bertone swaying from side to side and joining in on the "Glory, glory, hallelujah," and I couldn't help wondering what he would have thought of the other words to that militant song.

After the ceremony on the South Lawn, the pope and the president withdrew for a private conversation while Archbishop Sambi and I accompanied Cardinal Bertone and Secretary Rice to their tête-à-tête in the Cabinet Room of the White House. Secretary Rice did most of the talking. She initiated a discussion about the need for peace in the Middle East, about which no one disagreed, and explained the administration's hopes for a two-state solution. She seemed to be testing whether the United States might count on Holy See support. Cardinal Bertone was noncommittal. I left with the feeling that the Holy See had made a poor showing, and I wondered why the cardinal had not raised topics of his own and what his concept of the purpose of the meeting had been. And, once again, I wondered why Pope Benedict had chosen a man with no previous experience in diplomacy or foreign affairs to be his secretary of state.

That evening there was a gala dinner at the White House to celebrate the pope's visit. Pope Benedict himself had gone on to the next phase of his journey, a meeting with the entire body of the United States Bishops—about three hundred strong—at the Basilica of the National Shrine of the Immaculate Conception, where he spoke at length on the painful subject of sexual abuse of minors by members of the clergy. He reiterated what he had said on the plane about the need for the Church in America to reflect on the challenges ahead. Again, he praised the United States as a model of a secular state where many religions have not only coexisted in relative harmony but actually flourished. He noted approvingly that, historically, Americans "do not hesitate to bring moral arguments rooted in biblical faith into their public discourse."[21] The two most important challenges for the Church in America, he told the bishops, were the advance of relativism and a negative form of secularism characterized by hostility to religion.

Meanwhile, at the White House dinner, President Bush was trying to help Senator McCain's presidential campaign by introducing him to dozens of Catholic leaders. The hope was that they would get to know the senator better and that he would have a chance to learn more about the concerns of Catholics. George Bush, a Methodist, was quite conversant with Catholic social thought. He could "speak Catholic" with ease and seemed to like doing so. Senator John Kerry, who lost the Catholic vote to Bush by five points in 2004, did not have that ability. Neither did John McCain.

The president had seated me between himself and McCain,

with Mary Towey on McCain's other side. Mary and her husband, Jim, had worked for a number of years with Mother Teresa and were very familiar with all aspects of Catholic charities. Another guest was Carl Anderson, who led one of the world's largest charitable organizations, the Knights of Columbus, which has almost 2 million members. Over dinner a number of us spoke about the roles of government and faith-based initiatives in getting aid into the hands of the people who needed it most, a topic that one would have expected to rouse the interest of a presidential candidate. We spoke of the president's initiatives in that area and discussed how religious and other private charitable groups could often deliver social services, education, and health care more economically, effectively, and humanely than government. Carl Anderson was at his thoughtful and eloquent best as he tried without success to draw McCain into the conversation.

Senator McCain, unlike Cardinal Bertone, did not have an inscrutable public face. He appeared bored and indifferent as he toyed with his meal. He asked no questions, launched no topics of his own, and rushed away as soon as the dinner ended. It was no surprise to me when McCain lost the Catholic vote by nine points that year.

On the third day of the pope's visit, he celebrated Mass in Nationals Park, the home of Washington's major league baseball team. This was a special occasion for me because it gave me a chance to thank a person who had played an important role in my life and in the lives of countless other girls and boys in Dalton. Our sixth-grade teacher, Miss Mary Flynn, had opened our eyes to the world beyond Berkshire County. She introduced us to the wonders of ancient Greece and Rome, to the thrill of the Italian opera, to the founding principles of our government, and to the role of little townships like ours in that grand design.

Miss Flynn had written me that spring to say that while she had made pilgrimages to Rome to attend Masses celebrated by Popes Pius XII, John XXIII, Paul VI, and John Paul II, she was now unable at age eighty-eight to stand for a long time in the crowd at one of Pope Benedict's Masses in the United States. That was a problem I could solve. I arranged for her to sit with me in the ambassadors' box, where she, as a pro-life Democrat, was almost as excited to meet my friend Ambassador Ray Flynn (former Mayor of Boston) as she was to see Pope Benedict.

The next day, I flew to New York to attend the pope's speech to the United Nations General Assembly. The auditorium was packed to overflowing.

The pope gave about a third of his speech in French and then switched to English. Returning to a major theme of his American trip, he devoted part of his remarks to the defense of a capacious concept of religious freedom. "It is inconceivable," he said, "that believers should have to suppress a part of themselves—their faith—in order to be active citizens." He went on to advocate for the expansive definition of religious freedom in Article 18 of the Universal Declaration of Human Rights:

It should never be necessary to deny God in order to enjoy one's rights. The rights associated with religion are the more in need of protection if they are considered to clash with a prevailing secular ideology or with majority religious positions of an exclusive nature. The full guarantee of religious liberty cannot be limited to the free exercise of worship, but has to give due consideration to the public dimension of religion and hence to the possibility of believers playing their part in building the social order.[22]

When he finished, the assembled diplomats rose to give him a prolonged standing ovation. Such displays of appreciation for the words of a pope might seem puzzling, given the scant evidence that the UN or its members take any of these papal messages to heart. But in the UN setting, I have often noticed that papal envoys, too, generally receive an attentive hearing. Perhaps that is because the other diplomats know that Holy See representatives are charged to speak and act for the good of humanity—not just for the sovereign entity they represent, and not just for Catholics. As Cardinal Tauran once described their mission: "Our duty is to promote and defend not only the freedom and rights of Catholic communities around the world, but also to promote certain principles without which there is no civilization." In recent years, unfortunately, much of the Holy See's influence as a moral voice on the international stage has been lost due to its relative silence on human rights abuses in such places as China, Cuba, Hong Kong, and Venezuela.

On the day after his UN speech, Pope Benedict celebrated Mass in St. Patrick's Cathedral, where he elaborated on his exhortation to the American bishops to make known the richness of the Catholic vision. Pointing to the cathedral's stained-glass windows, he noted that many writers, including Nathaniel Hawthorne, had used the image of stained glass to illustrate the mystery of the Church herself. "It is only from the inside, from the experience of faith and ecclesial life," he said, "that we see the Church as she truly is: flooded with grace, resplendent in beauty, adorned by the manifold gifts of the Spirit."[23]

Only two months later, President Bush made a return visit to Pope Benedict. The visit was part of a European trip designed to strengthen the transatlantic partnership and to commemorate the sixtieth anniversary of the Marshall Plan and the Berlin Airlift. The meeting between the president and the pope was remarkable because it was their third encounter within a little over a year, the first having taken place at the Vatican in June 2007. No other U.S. president had ever consulted so frequently with a pope.

Security concerns, naturally, ran high while the president was in Rome, and preparation for the visit involved intense collaboration among the Vatican Gendarmerie Corps,[24] the FBI, and the Secret Service. But even when not on special alert, we at the embassy had constant reminders that both the Holy See and U.S. installations in Rome were prime targets for terrorist attack. As the head of the gendarmerie, Domenico Giani, explained while briefing me and FBI Director Robert Mueller, there are three reasons that many terrorist organizations have their eyes on Vatican City and especially the Basilica of Saint Peter: the symbolic value of the site, the softness of the target, and the fact that Americans constitute a large proportion of the nearly 4 million annual visitors to the Vatican.

The Holy See took particular care to give the Bushes a welcome that would show the pope's gratitude for the warm reception he had been given at the White House in April. Unlike the grand affair on the South Lawn, however, the meeting in Vatican City was more intimate. According to Vatican officials who spoke to Massimo Franco at the Italian newspaper *Corriere della Sera,* it was President Bush who suggested that the meeting should be of an informal nature. Some of the prelates interviewed "wondered why the President of the United States would make such a request."[25] Some speculated that this Protestant, who "spoke Catholic" so well, might be planning to cross the Tiber after he left office. My own view was that the outgoing, born-again Texan and the shy, retiring theologian had developed a genuine regard for each other and simply wished to speak freely for once.

Ordinarily, Pope Benedict received heads of state in his private library in the Apostolic Palace, but on this occasion the meeting was held in a special setting. The Torre San Giovanni is a round stone tower attached to the medieval wall surrounding Vatican City at the high westernmost end of the Vatican gardens.

When the Bushes and I arrived at the tower, the pope himself was standing at the door to greet us, smiling like any genial host. The two men withdrew to a studio on the top floor, while Laura Bush and I had the chance for a chat in the salon.

I told the first lady how grateful I was, as the mother of three daughters, for the way she conducted herself in public life. After a time, the pope and the president descended and continued their talk on a stroll through the Vatican gardens. Their destination was the spiritual heart of the gardens, the Lourdes Grotto, an exact replica of the grotto at Lourdes where the Virgin Mary had appeared to Saint Bernadette. There we were invited to sit while the Sistine Chapel choir sang *Exultate Deo* and *Alma Redemtoris Mater.*

That afternoon the president sent me a note from Air

The papal welcome at the entrance to the Torre San Giovanni

Force One, saying how much he enjoyed the visit and that "today was a very special day." From Pope Benedict's relaxed and smiling demeanor, I judged that he had felt the same.

But according to *La Repubblica*'s Vaticanista, Orazio la Rocca, the unusual courtesies extended to the president had given rise to "disgruntled murmurings" from some members of the curia, who viewed the pope's welcome to the president as *"troppo calorosa"* (too warm).[26] "More than a few prelates," la Rocca wrote, "do not understand why so much warmth is being extended to a person who, from the historical-political point of view, is basically very far from papal exhortations concerning peace and condemning war." Indeed, said la Rocca, many curial officials expressed "surprise and discomfort" at the exceptional care that was taken to make the visit a memorable one for the Bushes—the walk in the gardens, the visit to the shrine of our Lady, the concert in the grotto.

"Incomprehensible, all these attentions," said one anonymous cardinal, while others noted that papal audiences had recently been denied to other visiting heads of state.

But the courtesies extended by the pope to President Bush were not hard to understand. They liked each other. Even before they had met, and shortly after Benedict's election to the papacy, President Bush had told those attending a Catholic prayer breakfast that "Catholics and non-Catholics alike can take heart in the man who sits on the chair of Saint Peter, because he speaks with affection about the American model of liberty rooted in moral conviction."[27]

As Massimo Franco put it, the rapport between Benedict XVI and George W. Bush was "strikingly harmonious." Francis X. Rocca, a longtime Vatican watcher for *The Wall Street Journal,* agreed that the bond between the two was personal as well as political. Looking back at their April meeting in Washington, he wrote, "Nowhere has the congruence of their thinking been clearer than at April's welcoming ceremony at the White House when Bush cited Benedict's denunciation of the 'dictatorship of relativism,' and the Pope noted the importance of American religiosity as inspiration for abolitionism and the civil rights movement."[28]

As for me, I felt fortunate that my tenure as ambassador coincided with a time when the unique partnership between the United States and the Holy See was especially close.

CHAPTER EIGHT

Public Diplomacy 24/7

✤

There is still a central role for public diplomacy. . . . Today's
world of instant communication, viral amplification and
polarized platforms makes public diplomacy both more
complex and more important than ever.

—American diplomat WINSTON LORD[29]

During my term as ambassador, the chief business of Embassy Vatican was public diplomacy, and the same was true of the Holy See, where Pope Benedict himself was the chief public diplomat. While sitting in the audience when the pope addressed the UN General Assembly in April 2008, I was bemused to recall that many Vatican observers had doubted whether Joseph Ratzinger as pope would be able to communicate effectively to diverse audiences in the public square. It is one thing, they said, to be a star in the field of theology, and another to hold the attention of worldly listeners in such places as the British Parliament at Westminster, the German Bundestag, the Élysée Palace, the White House, and the United Nations. Yet Pope Benedict's speeches in those centers of power are now counted among his best.[30] Few had imagined that the reserved elderly theologian could step so easily into the limelight, or that his speeches on the great themes of human rights, religious freedom, and the synergy between faith and reason would make such a deep impression on many secular minds. Pope Benedict's UN speech made it clear that he, like his predecessor, was going to use his public platform to be a global moral witness.

That day at the UN, I could not help wondering whether the diplomats who applauded the pope so vigorously had really grasped the full implications of his words. Up to a point, there was much continuity with what previous popes had said about the post–World War II international human rights project. Like his predecessors, Pope Benedict praised the Universal Declaration of Human Rights, and credited it with having enabled "different cultures, juridical expressions and institutional models to converge around a fundamental nucleus of values and hence of rights."[31] Indeed, he noted, human rights had increasingly become "the common language and ethical substratum of international relations."

That is precisely what human rights advocates in the immediate postwar years had hoped for, and what skeptics had said would never happen. Political "realists" had scoffed at the idea that mere words in a nonbinding document could make a difference. But by 1989, people around the world were marveling that a few simple words of truth—and a few courageous people willing to call good and evil by name—could help to change the course of history.

Many of the pope's listeners must have been surprised, therefore, to hear him launch into the most sobering cautionary discussion about human rights that has ever appeared in any papal statement. He mentioned no fewer than ten threats that had menaced the human rights project from the beginning, and that were becoming ever more acute: cultural relativism, positivism, philosophical relativism, the unsettled question of foundations, utilitarianism, selective approaches to the common core of basic rights, escalating demands for new rights, hyperindividualistic interpretations of rights, neglect of the relation between rights and responsibilities, and the threat to religious freedom posed by dogmatic secularism.

That shift in papal tone reflected just how much had changed since the glory days of the international human rights movement. What hardly anyone had foreseen was that the more the human rights idea showed its power, the more intense would become the struggle to wield that power for various ends. It was an artist—as is so often the case—who sensed the danger before most other people did. Playwright-activist Václav Havel, watching the collapse of the Berlin Wall, had marveled at the power of words: "I really do inhabit a world where words are capable of shaking the entire system of government, where words can be mightier than ten military divisions."[32] But he warned that the same words that can make men free could also enslave them, and that sometimes the noblest human enterprises could be turned against themselves.

By the time of the UN's Cairo population conference in 1994 and the Beijing Conference on Women in 1995, what Havel had discerned in 1989 was plain to anyone who cared to notice. Special interest groups sought to harness the moral authority of the human rights idea to their agenda items, hoping to have them recognized as international human rights. A veritable human rights industry had arisen, and with changes in scale had come changes in ambition and emphasis. With great victories behind them, human rights activists searched for new causes. Dependence on Western funding often led to promoting ideas that were more popular in West-

ern societies than in other parts of the world—and more popular with wealthy donors in those societies than with their
fellow citizens.

To make matters worse, promoters of new rights often attacked established rights that did not suit their agendas, ig-
noring the principle that "all human rights are universal,
indivisible and interdependent and interrelated" (Vienna
Declaration, 1993). Some of the concepts of rights promoted
by Western activists prompted charges of cultural imperial-
ism in non-Western countries, while some of the world's
worst rights violators were using the argument of cultural
specificity to mask their transgressions.

In sum, by the time of Pope Benedict's UN address, the
international human rights project was in crisis. Questions
that the drafters of the Universal Declaration of Human
Rights had grappled with sixty years earlier had returned
with a vengeance: How can any rights be deemed universal in
a world of great cultural and political diversity? What happens when one fundamental right clashes with another?
What role should society, the state, and international bodies
play in enforcing rights?

As I thought about Pope Benedict's speech on the way back
to Rome, his frequent references to the upcoming sixtieth anniversary of the Universal Declaration of Human Rights convinced me that I had made the right decision when I made
human rights the central theme of the five-conference series I
was planning for 2008. What better way, I thought, to commemorate twenty-five years of formal diplomatic relations
between the United States and the Holy See than to gather
the diplomatic community for discussion of current challenges to ideals they had all formally endorsed?

The Anniversary Conference Series

The conference series also turned out to be a way to deepen relationships with other embassies. Because of the large presence of Latin American diplomats in Rome and of Latin American officials within the Vatican, I was particularly keen to launch our series with a symposium on the little-known but crucial Latin American contributions to the post–World War II international human rights project. While researching the history of the Universal Declaration for *A World Made New,* I had discovered that Latin American nations had been a driving force in that project, making sure that human rights were not ignored by the "Big Three"—the United States, Great Britain, and the Soviet Union—in their planning for a postwar future.

As the largest single bloc in the early UN (twenty of the original fifty countries), they had considerable clout, and they used it. At the UN founding conference in 1945, they took the lead in insisting on the inclusion of human rights references in the UN Charter.[33] And when the declaration was being debated in 1948, Latin American delegates again played key roles in the process. Since this fascinating part of human rights history had been nearly forgotten, even in Latin America, we seized the opportunity to make it better known.

The conference was well attended, which augured well for the rest of our series. The staff and I were excited to spot several Holy See officials, ambassadors, and Italian political figures among over two hundred attendees. The elderly Giulio Andreotti, former Italian prime minister and longtime leader of the Christian Democratic Party, sat attentively in the front row.

For our second event, the choice to highlight the joint efforts of the United States and the Holy See to combat human trafficking was an easy one. My predecessors, Ambassadors Jim Nicholson and Francis Rooney, had established a fruitful collaboration with the Italian Union of Major Superiors to assist women religious from around the world in forging networks to combat that modern form of slavery in countries of origin, transit, and destination. We presented the highlights of what was being accomplished, featuring personal testimonies from women who had been assisted and the women who had helped them. The conference ended with the announcement that the leaders of the Italian union of male religious would be joining the initiative.

The third event in our series focused on one of the most important areas of common interest between the United States and the Holy See—their shared commitment to the relief of poverty, hunger, and disease among the poorest people in the poorest parts of the world. On those fronts, a strong partnership had been formed between the United States, as the world's largest donor of humanitarian assistance, and the Holy See, as overseer of the world's largest network of providers of health care, education, and general aid to the poor.[34]

Pope Benedict had warned in his first encyclical, *Deus Caritas Est,* "God Is Love," against the notion, long common in Europe, that charity is primarily the responsibility of the state:

The state that would provide everything, absorbing everything into itself, would ultimately become a mere bureaucracy incapable of guaranteeing the very thing the suffering person—every person—needs: namely love and personal concern. We do not need a state that regulates and controls everything, but a state that, in accordance with the principle of subsidiarity, generously acknowledges and supports initiatives arising from the different social forces.[35]

A major purpose of this conference, "Philanthropy and Human Rights: Creating Space for *Caritas* in Civil Society," was to familiarize a European audience with the idea that many social services can be provided through the intermediate institutions of civil society more efficiently, economically, and humanely than through the state. To provide concrete illustrations of mixed private and public approaches, our embassy brought together experts representing the combined wisdom and experience of the American tradition of private generosity, the modern human rights tradition with its emphasis on the interdependence of social and economic rights and civil and political rights, and the tradition of Catholic social thought with its emphasis on solidarity, subsidiarity, and human dignity.

Our fourth program was designed with Pope Benedict's cautionary statements about human rights in mind. For this conference, " 'For Everyone, Everywhere': Universal Human Rights and the Challenge of Diversity," we asked human rights experts from Hong Kong, Japan, the Middle East, Italy, Norway, and the United States to discuss the current challenges facing the human rights project.

For a perspective from the Holy See, I invited Cardinal Renato Martino, who was then the president of the Pontifical Council for Justice and Peace, after a long ambassadorial service that had taken him to countries in Asia, Latin America, and the Middle East. He began his remarks by reminiscing about our time together in Beijing, as if we had always been the best of friends. And, in fact, by that time we sort of were.

The State Department ("Main State" as the embassy staff called it) was pleased with the press coverage the conference received, and it arranged for me to hold a worldwide web chat on the human rights crisis as part of the department's own celebration of the anniversary of the Universal Declaration of Human Rights later that year.

The grand finale of our yearlong series was the celebration of the twenty-fifth anniversary of diplomatic relations between the United States and the Holy See. For this gala event, we chose one of Rome's most beautiful settings, the historic Villa Aurelia, a grand seventeenth-century palazzo situated high on the Janiculum Hill and surrounded by eleven acres of gardens.

The topic, "The American Model of Religious Freedom," was chosen in response to a flood of questions we had received over the course of the year. Throughout 2008, Pope Benedict had made religious freedom the theme of several speeches, emphasizing a concept he called "positive secularism" and citing "the American model" as his prime example. Both of those terms caused considerable puzzlement in different quarters. For some Catholics, it was unsettling to hear a pope saying good things about secularism, even if he did put the word *positive* in front of it. His praise of a form of secularism was equally disconcerting to militant secularists (who saw it as a bid to capture a word they thought they owned). And in some precincts of the papal court, the pope's repeated praise of an American model was harder to take than his promotion of a form of secularism.

At Embassy Vatican, we were besieged with requests to explain just what this American model was that the pope was always talking about. American church-state law was terra incognita to most Italian politicians, intellectuals, and members of the diplomatic corps. (And no wonder, since if there is one thing on which constitutional scholars in the United States agree, it is that religion-clause jurisprudence is one of the most complex and confusing areas of constitutional law.)

I had already decided at the beginning of our planning process to make religious freedom the subject of our final conference, and now it was clear that the focus should be on the distinctive American system.

Public Diplomacy on the Road

I was also fortunate that my previous work in the field of human rights led to many opportunities for public diplomacy in European venues. One was an invitation from Václav Havel to deliver the keynote address at the annual conference of the Prague Forum 2000, the organization he had founded to support democratic principles, promote respect for human rights, assist the development of civil society, and encourage religious, cultural, and ethnic tolerance. That invitation was especially meaningful to me because Havel's speeches and writings had been a major inspiration for my book *Rights Talk*, on the impoverishment of political discourse.

At the Prague event, I took the occasion to make a plea for the recovery of the sense of the Universal Declaration of Human Rights as a unified body of principles that were meant to be read together, not as a menu from which one can choose only one's favorites. Since concerns about the Euro-

With Václav Havel at the 2008 meeting of the Prague Forum 2000

pean Union's reach into national affairs were percolating in the Czech Republic, I also focused on the fact that the framers of the declaration had taken for granted that its fertile principles could be brought to life in different cultures in a legitimate variety of ways.[36] They had endowed it with an integrated structure that was flexible enough to allow for some differences in emphasis and implementation, though not so malleable as to permit any basic right to be completely eclipsed.

Fortuitously, the publication that year of the Italian translation of my collected essays brought several other opportunities to promote the interests and values of the United States. Invitations to give speeches took me to many venues in Rome and to parts of Italy I had not visited before—the island of Capri with its breathtaking vistas, the Tuscan seaside town of Capalbio (the Martha's Vineyard of the Italian left), the commune of Bassano del Grappa (famed for its Alpine soldiers and strong brandy), and the annual Comunio e Liberazione festival, which draws nearly eight hundred thousand visitors each year to Federico Fellini's hometown of Rimini on the Adriatic.

In Bassano, I encountered an experiment in education for democracy that deserves to be better known. In 1962, the elders of this picturesque commune in the southeastern Alps founded an association called the Comune dei Giovani (Commune of the Young People). Designed to prepare young men and women for active and informed Christian citizenship, the group is organized like a real Italian commune. Its mayor, deputy mayor, and ministers for finance, culture, social commitment, religious education, and recreational activities are elected by the members, and the young people themselves are responsible for fundraising and administration. Over the years, many of them have gone on to hold public office in Bassano and elsewhere.

On those trips within Italy, for security reasons, I was always accompanied by Roman plainclothes policemen. Strictly speaking, though, *plainclothes* isn't the best term for Italian officers out of uniform. I learned that from Suzanne Nicholson's account of the first time she and her husband, former Ambassador Jim Nicholson, arranged to meet their escorts early one morning to go running. At the appointed hour, Suzanne and Jim showed up in the old sweat suits they used for exercise and found their Roman escorts ready to go—in Gucci running gear! I had a similar experience while shopping for Christmas gifts. I had been told of a store near the Pantheon where one could buy Italian silk neckties at a reasonable price. On the way, I asked my escort if he had ever bought anything there. "No," he said, "I only wear Valentino."

On most of these speaking engagements, I was also accompanied by Lucia Tedeschi, an elegant Italian woman engaged by the embassy to provide Italian conversation on a regular basis with any officer who wished to have that service. Lucia and I quickly discovered many common interests and became friends. She would arrive at my office, high heels clicking on the parquet, with a folder full of newspaper items to discuss and photocopies of novellas or short stories to read later on. We would talk about everything under the sun while she corrected my grammar.

During the Cold War years, Lucia had lived with her journalist husband in Vienna, moving back to Rome after his death. Given Vienna's strategic position between East and West, and given that there is such a fine line between journalism and spying, and given that she was fluent in English, French, and German as well as Italian, I imagined her previous life as romantic and dangerous. One day I asked Lucia about her unusual menswear jackets with collars and cuffs of flowered silk. She told me that the jackets had belonged to her late husband and that she had had them altered and embellished for her own use. I do not know whether that was a way of remaining close to her husband, an economy measure, a personal fashion statement, or all three, but it was a unique and glamorous look. Since I had to give many speeches in Italian, I was immensely grateful to Lucia not only for polishing my texts but for coming often, on her own time, to hear me speak.

In Rome itself there was so much interest in Pope Benedict's concept of positive secularism that Cardinal Camillo Ruini, the Vicar General of the Diocese of Rome, and I were asked to have a public discussion on the subject of American and European models of religious freedom in the magnificent Palazzo Colonna, site of one of the largest private art collections in Italy. I was both excited and a little nervous at the prospect of an exchange with Cardinal Ruini. A former president of the Italian Bishops' Conference, he was an impressive speaker, equally at home in the realms of politics and academic discourse. But I had no idea how he regarded the pope's enthusiasm for the American model. Even though I was quite familiar with the topic, I worked harder on preparing my speech for that evening than on any other talk I gave that year.

On the appointed day, the cardinal and I were led by Prince Prospero Colonna through a gallery of paintings by Ghirlandaio, Tintoretto, Carracci, and Reni to the palazzo's Sala Grande, with its enormous ceiling fresco commemorating the Battle of Lepanto, where the combined Christian fleet (with Marcantonio Colonna as deputy commander) defeated the fleet of the Ottoman Empire in 1571.

Since it was the mysterious American model that most needed to be explained, I was the leadoff speaker. As an American, I said, I had felt a certain patriotic pride when I first heard Pope Benedict speak so warmly of the United States as a model of "positive secularism." It seemed that what intrigued the pope, like Tocqueville before him, was that the American founders had insisted on the distinction between the religious and political spheres, but had done so out of respect for religion, in order to protect it from the state. And like Tocqueville, Benedict saw the United States as an example of how such an approach could benefit both religion and society. He contrasted the path taken by the Americans with that of France, where a negative form of secularism, aimed at protecting the state from religion, was born of Enlightenment hubris and revolutionary fury.[37]

The pope had sounded that theme many times that year. On his visit to the United States, he expressed his appreciation for "a nation that welcomes the role of religion in the public square" and for being a model of a secular state where many religions coexist in relative harmony.[38] Upon his return to Italy, he spoke of American society as characterized by a "healthy secularism" through which "the religious dimension, with the diversity of its expressions, is not only tolerated but appreciated as the nation's 'soul' and as a fundamental guarantee of human rights and duties."[39]

I told our Roman audience that while it had been pleasant to hear those words, they had made me uneasy at first because the very features of my country's system that the pope admired had been eroded. But when Pope Benedict met with the U.S. bishops, it was evident he was keenly aware that the American model was in trouble, weakened by changes in the culture, and under assault on many fronts. He warned the bishops not to ignore the growing threat of a form of secularism that allows for professing belief in God but that confines faith to the private sphere and encourages the separation of faith from the rest of life. Neither should they take America's traditional religiosity for granted and "go about business as usual, even as its foundations are being slowly undermined."[40]

It was clear, I said, that the pope's praise of the "American model" in the United States was intended to remind his

American audience of the advantages of the system their founders had devised and to inspire them to preserve one of their greatest treasures. I described how that model had been modified by judicial interpretation, and I concluded with a discussion of some current controversies.

Cardinal Ruini discussed the form of secularism in France and some other European countries, which he called the French Model. The grandfatherly prelate knew his audience well. In pre-Revolutionary France, he said, an unhealthy entanglement of religion and politics had led to a concept of secularism that was hostile to religion. Yet President Nicolas Sarkozy had surprised everyone the preceding month by endorsing Pope Benedict's concept of positive secularism. Perhaps, the cardinal suggested, a change was brewing even in the cradle of *laïcité*. A better model for Europe, he suggested, would be Italy, where the Catholic religion is distinct, but not wholly separated, from the state, and where Catholics, persons of other faiths, and persons of no faith can all participate in public life without checking their beliefs at the door.[41]

Within the U.S. State Department, as 2008 came to a close, there was a sense of impending change where religion was concerned. That the bureaucracy was preparing for a new administration was apparent at the annual Christmas tree-lighting ceremony for employees of the three U.S. embassies in Rome: the embassies to Italy, the Holy See, and the United Nations Food and Agriculture Organization (FAO). The event, held at Embassy Rome on the Via Veneto, was a brief affair. The tree was lit; children sang some songs about reindeer, holly, and sleigh bells; and each of the three ambassadors delivered short remarks. From the talks by the ambassadors to Italy and the FAO, which were almost certainly drafted by State Department employees, no bystander would know that a religious holiday was being celebrated. As the last speaker, I did my best to fill the gap, taking my cue from the heartfelt words about the nativity that President Bush had spoken a few days earlier at the White House Christmas ceremony: "The simple story we remember during the season speaks to every generation. It is the story of a humble birth in a quiet town and the story of one life that changed millions more. For two millennia, the story of Christmas has brought joy to families, comfort to communities, and hope to hearts around the world."

With the Bush administration at its end, my term of service ended as well. It remained only for me to pay farewell visits to Pope Benedict, Cardinal Bertone, and the various officials of the Second Section of the Secretariat of State with whom I had interacted over the year. The Holy See diplomats seemed cautiously optimistic about the new administration in the United States, hoping that there might be new opportunities for diplomacy with regard to the Middle East and Cuba. At the same time, they expressed concern about possible linkage of U.S. foreign aid to aggressive population-control policies and possible infringements of religious freedom and conscience rights. We all shared the view that the election of an African American to the presidency spoke well for the state of race relations in the United States.

I returned to academic life in January 2009 with gratitude for the privilege of serving in a period when relations between the United States and the Vatican had been amicable, and with eagerness to pick up where I had left off. In the summer of 2007, when I had spoken about the duties of an ambassador with former Holy See Ambassadors Ray Flynn,

Francis Rooney, and Jim Nicholson, they all assured me that I would have plenty of time for writing. State Department officials said the same, pointing out that staff members would be providing me with drafts of speeches, reports, and memoranda. But as I was not comfortable with giving speeches that I did not write myself, the only writing I got done in Rome was on speeches and reports. I was impatiently looking forward, therefore, to the quiet life of a law professor. Having resigned all my positions with the Holy See, I expected that my service in that venue would be confined to the Pontifical Academy of Social Sciences, if I were reappointed. No sooner did I get home, however, than I found myself in the midst of a controversy.

CHAPTER NINE

Rumble at Notre Dame; Woes for a New Pope

✤

Repose is not the destiny of man.

—OLIVER WENDELL HOLMES JR., *The Path of the Law*

Shortly before leaving Rome in January 2009, I received a phone call from the president of the University of Notre Dame, Rev. John I. Jenkins, informing me that I had been selected to receive the university's annual Laetare Medal "in recognition of outstanding service to the Catholic Church and society." I was thrilled at being chosen for such a great honor from one of the nation's finest universities. I readily accepted and began jotting down some ideas for an acceptance speech. Then in March, President Jenkins called me again, this time to say he had "great news"—the president of the United States would be giving that year's commencement speech. That was good, I said, and started revising my remarks for an occasion where I would be sharing the podium with Barack Obama, whom I recalled as a likable young man in my first-year property class at Harvard. Then came the news that Notre Dame would be giving President Obama an honorary degree.

That may sound of little consequence, but it put me in a difficult situation. The U.S. Conference of Catholic Bishops (USCCB) had expressly requested Catholic institutions not to "honor those who act in defiance of our fundamental moral principles," specifying that such persons "should not be given awards, honors or platforms which would suggest support for their actions." The bishops' position seemed to me eminently reasonable: it left Catholic institutions completely free to invite, listen to, and engage with anyone they wished, so long as they did not confer honors on people whose actions were in direct contradiction to basic moral principles. Notre Dame's decision to disregard that guideline by honoring a prominent abortion rights advocate greatly complicated the writing of my little speech, especially since I was a longtime consultant to the USCCB.

Then things got worse. Notre Dame, in an attempt to pacify irate alumni and others who objected to the honorary degree, issued a set of "talking points," implying that my brief acceptance remarks would somehow "balance" the event: "President Obama won't be doing all the talking. Mary Ann Glendon, the former U.S. Ambassador to the Vatican, will be speaking as the recipient of the Laetare Medal."

That turned a difficult situation into an impossible one. As I wrote to President Jenkins, a commencement "is supposed to be a joyous day for the graduates and their families. It is not the right place, nor is a brief acceptance speech the right vehicle, for engagement with the very serious problems raised by Notre Dame's decision—in disregard of the settled position of the U.S. bishops—to honor a prominent and uncompromising opponent of the Church's position on issues involving fundamental principles of justice."

After I withdrew from the event, I was barraged for weeks with phone messages and letters from perfect strangers, for and against my decision. What bothered me most were letters praising or blaming me for what I didn't do. As I made clear in my letter declining the medal, I had no problem with Notre Dame inviting the president of the United States to give the commencement speech. My belief, both then and especially now, in this time of danger for free speech, is that Catholic universities should be models for the free exchange of ideas, inviting whomever they wish for robust and respectful discussion.

My return to the Pontifical Academy that spring was also less peaceful than I would have liked. I had been reappointed its president by Pope Benedict, and it was good to meet him again in that setting as we exchanged opening remarks at a plenary session on Catholic social doctrine and human rights. But all was not well in the Casina Pio IV. In a decision that I came to see as a mistake, the pope had left the academy's presidency vacant while I was serving as ambassador to the Holy See. In that interval, the behavior of the Argentinian bishop serving as the group's chancellor, Marcelo Sánchez Sorondo, had become more aberrant.

I was especially concerned when Paulus Zulu, the academy's only member from sub-Saharan Africa, told me he was going to resign because of Bishop Sánchez's disrespectful attitude toward him. Paulus was a mainstay of the academy whose journey through life had taken him from his youth under the apartheid regime in South Africa, to partisanship with Nelson Mandela, to disillusionment with the government of the African National Congress, to caring in his eighties for the young children of relatives who had died of complications from AIDS. When I pleaded with him to remain, he agreed, but the problem continued. And Paulus was not the only person to complain. Others bristled at the chancellor's Uriah Heep–like behavior: overbearing toward those whom he thought had nothing to offer him, and obsequious toward superiors.

On the scientific front, the academy had several promising projects under way. The economic crisis that had erupted in 2007, and that was still sending shock waves through the economies of many nations, held implications for many of the issues the group had studied over the years—especially labor and intergenerational solidarity. So it was decided to devote the 2010 plenary to "Crisis in the Global Economy," with a program that focused on current events to a greater degree than our previous conferences. The topic chosen for the following year, "Universal Rights in a World of Diversity: The Case of Religious Freedom," was, of course, of great interest to Pope Benedict, who sent us immediate encouragement and once again made religious freedom a central theme of his own speeches in the months leading up to the 2011 meeting.

The 2012 plenary commemorating Pope John XXIII's encyclical *Pacem in Terris,* however, was marred by peculiar behavior by Bishop Sánchez. As part of my efforts to increase public awareness of the academy's work and publications, I had engaged Father Raymond de Souza, a Canadian priest and journalist, to serve as press liaison at several of our conferences. His background in economics suited him well for the job, and his media experience was valuable in arranging interviews when we had high-profile guests. I was puzzled, therefore, when Bishop Sánchez told me that he no longer wanted Father de Souza to come to our meetings. When I asked why, he said that "some people," including the official spokesman for the Holy See, Father Federico Lombardi, had objected to de Souza's presence at our meetings "because he was not a member of the academy." That sounded so odd that I immediately walked over to the Vatican's press office to ask Father Lombardi, a longtime acquaintance, what his problem was with Father de Souza. There was no problem at all, he said, adding that, on the contrary, de Souza's presence had always been very helpful to him. It began to seem as though "some people" might be Sánchez himself, who regarded Father de Souza as too conservative.

As the time for the plenary session approached, Bishop Sánchez consulted me about the press conference that we usually held at the end of our meetings. Pointing out that the Holy See press office would be closed on May 1, the day our meeting ended, he suggested that we cancel the press conference that year, to which I agreed. Imagine my surprise when I learned that Bishop Sánchez held a press conference himself the day after I had departed from Rome. In addition, he had distributed a document to the press titled "Final Statement," as though it represented the conclusions of the academy. This was the man who was in charge, alone, of counting the members' ballots for new academicians, as well as of the academy's purse strings.

The matter of the unauthorized press conference and statement was serious enough that I felt I had to bring it to the attention of an official in the Secretariat of State. The problems with the eccentric bishop were nothing new to him. He sighed and offered no solution. I now know that he had his hands full with worse problems in other parts of the Vatican.

So far as the academy's future projects were concerned, it seemed to me that there was an urgent need for attention to

Catholic international relations theory. The Holy See had long been a strong supporter of the United Nations and other international bodies. But as Archbishop Augustine Di Noia, who was adjunct secretary of the Congregation for the Doctrine of the Faith, had pointed out at one of our meetings, the programs and policies of many international organizations, including the United Nations, had been profoundly influenced by a secular anthropology that "espouses the socially constructed character of truth and reality, the priority of cultural diversity, the deconstruction of all moral norms, and the priority of personal choice."[42] That constellation of views, with its hold on the media, international agencies, and other influential bodies, he continued, "created many practical problems that sometimes make it difficult for Catholic aid agencies even to function at the local, national, and even international levels." Without mincing words, Di Noia challenged the academicians, saying, "Although the roots of this secular anthropology are philosophical, the social sciences have been the principal vehicle for its diffusion in modern western societies."

Clearly, the time was overdue for Catholic international relations theorists to undertake a critical evaluation of the whole field, including the accomplishments, failures, and biases of contemporary international organizations. To what extent do they operate in accordance with the principle of subsidiarity? To what extent do they displace smaller structures that enable men and women to have a voice in setting the conditions under which they live, work, and raise their children? In their day-to-day activities, to what extent do they promote or impede freedom, solidarity, justice, security, and the pursuit of dignified living? Just as the Church cannot regard the nation-state as the final form of human political organization, it cannot assume that every group labeling itself "international" represents an advance for humanity.

Ex–Foreign Minister Cardinal Tauran, on whom I could always rely for wisdom, agreed with Di Noia. Over tea in his apartment, he went so far as to say he feared that the Vatican was in danger of becoming "just another NGO" rather than a distinctive moral voice in international settings.

I hoped the academy would follow up on those ideas, but since my second five-year term as president was due to expire in 2014, that would be a decision for others to make.

As I prepared to step down from the presidency of the academy, I had a reasonably good feeling about what had been accomplished. The membership had been strengthened by the addition of some prominent scholars with a good understanding of Catholic social thought. At its best, the group had helped to train the spotlight on the human dimensions of a wide range of social issues, bringing out spiritual and moral aspects that are too often ignored by purely secular social scientists. The volumes of the academy's proceedings contained some very fine essays by members and outside experts.

From the academy's beginning, however, it had seemed to me that structural defects in its organization would hamper its ability to fulfill the hopes of John Paul II for a body that would promote "the study and progress of the social sciences, primarily economics, sociology, law and political science." Without an academic director on the premises, a professional staff, and a budget for research, it was remarkable that such a diverse group was able to accomplish as much as it did.

It is possible that amendments to the Pontifical Academy

of Social Sciences statute, together with an adequate budget, could improve that body's ability to fulfill its assigned mission. But I am doubtful whether such a move would be wise, given limited resources and given the amount of good scholarship on Catholic social thought that is being carried out by lay and ecclesiastical experts at their own universities, think tanks, and associations around the world.

Moreover, many of the impediments to progress in the academy over the years were not unique to our little corner of the Vatican. Many were the results of failures in administration of which we were only dimly aware. Probably, we academicians, as social scientists, should have been more attuned to what happens in bureaucracies when departments are left with little supervision over a long period of time.

Neither John Paul II nor Benedict XVI had been a hands-on administrator. As even John Paul II's most admiring biographer, George Weigel, had to admit, administration was never his forte, even when he was Archbishop of Cracow.[43] Throughout the dramatic years when he played an instrumental role in the collapse of Eastern European communism, it was understandable that he would leave the heads of various departments more or less on their own. Then came illnesses and surgeries. Already in 1994, the very year the pope founded the academy, Diarmuid Martin described him to an interviewer for *The New Yorker* as "increasingly uninterested in details, in administration. There are issues far more important to him."

Pope John Paul II's mode of governing was to set large goals and to leave trusted people to pursue them. Much good was accomplished in this manner, but as Weigel wrote, the price of this mode of governing was that John Paul II left behind "a central administrative apparatus in which a minority of the personnel have internalized the dynamic teaching of his pontificate" but "where his vision of an evangelically assertive, culture-forming Church is not understood and shared throughout the bureaucracy."[44]

Many Catholics were shocked when Pope Benedict announced that he would retire on February 28, 2013, the first pope to do so in six hundred years. All sorts of theories were offered about why he would do such a thing. But I found nothing surprising in his statement that "I have come to the certain knowledge that my strength, due to the burdens of age, is no longer suitable for properly administering the Petrine office."[45] Even from my limited vantage point, I could see that he must have been overwhelmed by the magnitude and variety of the disasters that were all coming to a head. Moreover, the men he had chosen for secretary of state and prefect of the Congregation for the Doctrine of the Faith, Cardinals Bertone and Levada, had not been particularly well prepared for the responsibilities of those offices.

I had been given a preview of some of the burdens the pope was facing when Cardinal Bertone asked me in the spring of 2010 to assemble and chair a five-person committee (to include a canon lawyer, a sovereign immunity expert, two experienced litigators, and myself) to oversee litigation against the Holy See in the U.S. courts. That litigation was being handled extremely well, brilliantly in fact, by California lawyer Jeffrey Lena and his team. They had prevailed in every single case, some involving millions of dollars, that had been brought against the Holy See and the Vatican Bank in the U.S. courts since the papacy of John Paul II. Lena was the perfect man for the job: fluent in Italian, equally at home in American,

Italian, and Vatican law, and a skilled litigator. But with a growing number of lawsuits in American courts—some involving commercial disputes, some the question of responsibility for supervision in sex abuse cases, and all challenging the Holy See's sovereign immunity—our committee thought the work might soon be more than a small firm could handle.

The committee's assignment was to assess the situation, keep track of current cases, assist the Holy See's American attorneys, and report annually to the Secretariat of State. After meeting with Lena and reviewing the current cases, the committee decided that the main immediate need was to have a major law firm with the requisite expertise for backup. That was easily arranged.

Of growing concern to the committee, however, was something that was not in our mandate: the fact that the Holy See, unlike other sovereigns, does not have anything resembling a centralized department to handle its legal affairs. Accordingly, one of the committee members, Anthony Picarello, general counsel and secretary of the U.S. Conference of Catholic Bishops, and I wrote to the new secretary of state, Cardinal Pietro Parolin, to advise that some sort of coordinating body would help to avert unnecessary litigation as well as oversee existing cases effectively. The absence of such a body, we pointed out, posed a continuing risk that actions and decisions in any one of the Holy See's departments might have adverse effects on legal matters in other departments. We illustrated our recommendation with a specific example of how that had already occurred in a recent case. Not only governments but large private organizations, we noted, have legal offices that handle crisis management, compliance reporting, public relations related to legal matters, and supervision of relations with outside legal consultants. We never received a reply.

I was heartened, therefore, when the new pope, Francis, announced that reform of the Church's central governing body, the curia, would be among his top priorities.

PART III

The Court of Pope Francis

Life in court society was not peaceful. The number of people permanently and inescapably bound to one circle was large. They pressed on each other, struggled for prestige, for their place in the hierarchy. The affairs, intrigues, conflicts over rank and favour knew no end. Everyone depended on everyone else, and all on the king. Each could harm each. He who rode high today was cast down tomorrow. There was no security. Everyone had to seek alliances with others whose stock was high, avoid unnecessary enmities, fight unavoidable enmities with cold calculation, and scrupulously maintain towards all others the degree of distance befitting their status.

—NORBERT ELIAS,
The Court Society

CHAPTER TEN

A Pope from the New World;
a Bank in Trouble

✢

*I think that the Curia has fallen somewhat from the level it
once had, in the days of the old curialists. . . . The profile of the
old curialist, faithful, doing his work. We need these people. . . .
There are some, but not as many as there once were.*

—POPE FRANCIS, four months after his election[1]

In April 2013, a month after the election of Pope Francis, the
Piazza San Pietro was still packed with TV cameras, pil-
grims, and casual onlookers. Members of the Pontifical Academy wove their way through the crowds toward the entrance
to Vatican City for our spring meeting. Our first stop was at
our lodgings in the Casa Santa Marta, where, we heard, the
latest resident took his meals in the common dining room
like everyone else except that he sat at a special table.

We were intensely curious about the new pope. Like most
of my colleagues in the academy, I saw it as a promising sign
that a non-European had been chosen. The time was right, I
thought, for a pope from Africa, Asia, or Latin America, a
pope whose presence would reflect the universality of the
church. But most of all I hoped that whoever he was and
wherever he came from, he would be the hands-on administrator that the Holy See so badly needed.

As usual, the academy's spring meeting began with an audience with the Holy Father. We were taken by bus to the Apostolic Palace, where we awaited Pope Francis's arrival in the Sala Clementina, with its dramatic fresco of the martyrdom of Pope Clement, who was cast into the sea with an anchor around his neck when Emperor Trajan got wind of his success in evangelization.

In the past, these meetings had begun with a formal exchange of remarks between the academy's president and the pope, and in the time of John Paul II they had included a personal greeting from the pope for each academician and guest speaker. But we were told that this encounter would be brief.

When Pope Francis entered the hall, I welcomed him on behalf of the academy and gave him a copy of the Argentinian Jesuit magazine *Criterio,* where his article *"No tenemos derecho a la indiferencia,"* that is, "We have no right to indifference," was next to the Spanish translation of an article I had written on the role of the laity.

Welcoming the newly elected Pope Francis to the Pontifical Academy

The pope sat down for a formal photo with the group, then rose, stood for a moment facing us, and said, "Well, good-bye." The brevity of the ceremony was disappointing to some, but we all understood that the new pontiff was just beginning to settle into his role. And there was something touching about his awkwardness, his uncertain smile, the way his papal sash, called a *fascia,* kept slipping out of place.

For the academy's chancellor, Bishop Sánchez, the new pontificate was a dream come true. My term as president would soon be over, and Pope Francis, a fellow Argentinian, would be far too busy to interfere with the bishop's efforts to bring the academy closer to his own vision of Catholic social thought—the vision that had brought him some notoriety in 2018 when he announced, to the chagrin of Vatican public relations personnel, "Those who best realize the social doctrine of the Church are the Chinese."[2]

The new pope had decided to live at the Casa Santa Marta, and it was not uncommon in those early days to see him coming and going around the place. It was an unspoken understanding that the other guests should leave him in peace, but occasionally he would stop to greet someone. One morning as I was on my way down to the dining room for breakfast, the elevator door opened on the second floor, and I found myself face-to-face with the Holy Father. He smiled and thanked me for my work, and I replied, half seriously, that it was a *"penitenza per i miei peccati"* (a penance for my sins). *"Ne abbiamo tutti un sacco"* ("We've all got a lot of those"), he said with a laugh.

It was encouraging to see that, in the months following his election, Pope Francis was starting to address some of the thorny problems that had accumulated over the years. He established a Commission for the Protection of Minors, and he turned his attention to the troubled Institute of Religious Works, commonly known as the Vatican Bank or the IOR (pronounced "Eeyore," like the name of the donkey in Winnie-the-Pooh). I followed these developments with interest, as they were related to the business of the committee overseeing legal matters involving the Holy See in the United States. With my responsibilities for the social science academy coming to an end, I expected that my service to the Holy See would be confined to that committee.

But a simmering pot was about to boil over in another part of the Vatican, and I was about to be drafted for another tour of duty. In the summer of 2013, Pope Francis appointed me to a five-person commission to assess the current state of the scandal-ridden Vatican Bank. Having chaired the Holy See's Committee on Litigation Against the Holy See in the United States, some of which involved the Vatican Bank, I was already familiar with some of the problems. And as I had done a good deal of work for one of America's largest banks as an associate at Chicago's Mayer, Brown & Platt, and had recently helped in the successful reorganization of two faltering nonprofit enterprises in the United States, I was intrigued.

Strictly speaking, the Vatican Bank is not a bank. It is a canonical foundation that provides financial services to a restricted clientele. In fact, its mission statement begins with the assertion that "the IOR is different from any other financial services provider" and goes on to explain that "the mission of the Institute is to serve the Catholic Church in all its forms . . . by holding and administering entrusted assets and providing dedicated payment services worldwide." But the popular name has passed into the language.

The Institute of Religious Works (the Vatican Bank)

The Vatican Bank's home, where I was to spend a good deal of time in the years ahead, is a gloomy-looking medieval tower that one passes after entering Vatican City from the Borgo Pio through the Santa Anna Gate. Its forbidding aspect is intensified by the shadows in that narrow street.

The institute's origins go back to the late nineteenth century, when Pope Leo XIII established a Commission for Works of Charity, but Pope Pius XII founded the IOR in its present form in 1942. At that turbulent moment, the Vatican had an urgent need for a reliable place to keep and invest the funds of religious organizations and for a safe way to get funds into the hands of missionaries and charitable agencies located in far-flung parts of the world. But as time went on, that unusual financial institution, that bank that was not a bank, attracted the attention of some very unsavory characters.

In 1974, the IOR lost an estimated $30 million through the machinations of a mafia-affiliated financial adviser, Michele

Sindona, who was later convicted of ordering the murder of a lawyer and then died in prison after drinking a cup of coffee laced with cyanide. The dark side of the institute's history also included a role in frauds that in 1982 led to the collapse of the Banco Ambrosiano, an Italian bank of which the IOR was the main shareholder. Dozens of individuals were convicted of financial crimes in the aftermath, and the Ambrosiano's chairman, Roberto Calvi, fled Italy to escape prosecution only to be found hanging from Blackfriars Bridge in London—a mystery that remains unsolved. The Ambrosiano scandal inspired the plot of *The Godfather Part III,* and, not surprisingly, references to the Vatican Bank became stock items in films and novels about crime, international intrigue, and the mafia.

The investigatory group to which I had been appointed, the Commission for Reference on the Institute of Religious Works, was quickly dubbed CRIOR. Our mandate was to conduct a thorough investigation of the past and present of the institute with a view toward determining whether it could be reformed or should be closed. Little knowing what lay ahead, I looked forward to the assignment. Overconfident American that I was, I thought all that was needed was for a few good people to roll up their sleeves and get to work. When one of my friends in the curia said, "Be careful, the Devil lives in the IOR," I thought he was joking.

CHAPTER ELEVEN

"The Devil Lives in the IOR"

✣

*He who travels in the Barque of Peter had better not
look too closely into the engine room.*

—THEOLOGIAN RONALD KNOX,
on being asked why he did not wish to go to Rome

No sooner had the Holy See announced that the pope had established the Commission for Reference on the Institute of Religious Works than headlines in the Italian press revealed why
such a body was urgently needed. Paolo Cipriani and Massimo
Tulli, the director and deputy director, respectively, of the IOR
suddenly resigned "in the best interests of the Holy See" after
a Vatican accountant already under investigation for money
laundering was arrested on charges of plotting to smuggle
20 million euros out of the country. Cipriani and Tulli were
later convicted of embezzlement and money laundering involving millions of euros' worth of illegal transactions.

If I could have foreseen how much of the next four and a
half years would be spent in often fruitless labor on the reform of the IOR, I would certainly have declined to step into
that quagmire. But I was optimistic about the possibility of
progress, Harvard was generous with time for outside legal
activities, and Edward encouraged me to take on what
sounded like a fascinating assignment. Moreover, the work
would afford many opportunities to spend time with my
daughter Liz and her family, who were based in Rome.

My optimism was not entirely unfounded. There were several reasons to think the CRIOR investigation could launch a process that would yield real results. During the pontificate of Benedict XVI, the IOR had already begun to bring its practices in line with international norms against terrorism and money laundering, as required by the European Monetary Convention, which the Holy See had signed in 2009. As part of that process, the Holy See had agreed to be reviewed by Moneyval, the Council of Europe's agency that evaluates smaller European states to determine their compliance with GAFI (Financial Action Group International) standards.

A further reason for hope was the composition of the commission itself. Cardinal Raffaele Farina, the Vatican librarian who would be CRIOR's president, was undoubtedly chosen for his impeccable reputation. The same was true of Cardinal Jean-Louis Tauran, who despite the advance of a form of Parkinson's disease was still one of the smartest and most respected members of the hierarchy. Monsignor Peter Wells, the American *assessore* for general affairs in the Secretariat of State, had a matchless knowledge of the administration of the Holy See and the Vatican City State. The group's coordinator, with whom I would be working closely, was Juan Ignacio Arrieta, a Spanish bishop serving as the secretary of the Pontifical Council for Legislative Texts, and a leading expert on canon law.

Most encouraging of all was the pope's chirograph, the apostolic letter establishing the commission. That document gave the CRIOR full powers to enter the IOR, to examine any materials, and to interview any employees and officers. Since the commission would need assistance from persons with specific kinds of expertise, the chirograph also authorized us to engage consultants.

Thus armed with a kind of general warrant, we took two early steps. Over the summer, Bishop Arrieta and I interviewed nearly every one of the 115 persons working in the IOR to obtain their confidential assessments of the institution. Second, we embedded an observer-investigator in the bank.

Prior to 2013, I had never set foot inside the Vatican's financial fiefdom. I got to know it rather well, however, while Arrieta and I were doing our interviews with its employees. Despite its forbidding aspect when viewed from the outside, the bank's interior is bright and well appointed—more like a boutique law firm with offices and conference rooms than a bank. But there was nothing bright or cheery about the statements we received from the men and women who worked there. Even though we explained to each interviewee that the pope himself had ordered the investigation and had stipulated that any information from the workforce must be held in absolute confidence, the atmosphere in the IOR was so permeated with fear and suspicion that most were nervous and mistrustful.

Many staff members were convinced that anything they said would get back to management and that they would suffer retribution. And management did in fact demand to see our material. But Arrieta kept everything well out of their reach and repelled every attempt to learn what we had been told.

By the time we finished our interviews, we had acquired much useful information about the present state of the IOR; the misdeeds of Cipriani and Tulli, as well as those of the staff members who had been close to those two; and day-to-day conditions in the workplace. Meanwhile, our indefatigable embedded consultant, Mario Clapis, was making dogged progress, despite heavy resistance to his requests for documents and information from Cipriani's successor.

From the beginning, our consultants were met with hostility by the senior management, which included a number of holdovers from the Cipriani-Tulli regime. Clapis was viewed as unnecessarily intrusive; attorney Jeffrey Lena had already earned the enmity of IOR management for having pushed for more aggressive anti-money-laundering reforms in connection with the Moneyval process; and Terrence Keeley, a BlackRock executive, was an independent American who dared to suspect that the IOR's actual financial condition did not square well with the rosy picture the IOR's public relations firm wanted to present.

That fall, after classes resumed at Harvard, I continued to work with Arrieta and the consultants by email and Skype. But suddenly, on October 5, 2013, my life changed forever. I had taken Edward to be treated for a minor infection at Beth Israel Hospital, where they decided to keep him overnight so that he could be given intravenous antibiotics. The next morning, I was getting ready to pick him up when a doctor called to tell me that my husband had died during the night. For the next several months, I was like a robot, performing necessary routines. A well-meaning friend gave me a copy of C. S. Lewis's *A Grief Observed*, which wasn't much comfort because nothing was, but I could identify with Lewis when he said, "At times it feels like being mildly drunk, or concussed. There is a sort of invisible blanket between the world and me. I find it hard to take in what anyone says. Or perhaps, hard to want to take it in. It is so uninteresting. Yet I want the others to be about me. I dread the moments when the house is empty."

Later on, recalling that period of grief and shock, I wondered whether I had made the right decision when I threw all my energy into work in the months that followed. I was not functioning at my best that fall as I went on teaching my classes and keeping in touch with what was going on in the CRIOR process. But the regularity of the classroom and the hope of contributing to the Church's much-needed reforms were a large part of what helped to keep me going.

By the time I returned to Rome, during the Thanksgiving break, our commission had accomplished a good deal in terms of getting a clear picture of the governance issues, the internal culture, and the financial condition of the IOR. The statements Arrieta and I had taken from the employees had told us almost everything we needed to know about the work environment and employee morale. Terry Keeley's assessment of the IOR's financial condition gave us reason to question the self-serving prognostications of management and to wonder whether the IOR was up to competing with modern financial institutions.

Where the IOR's governance was concerned, we ascertained that the 1990 statute that served as its constitutional framework was basically sound, though in need of updating. The bank's chronic problems were due not to any defect in the statute but to persistent failures to follow the statute. The governance of the IOR seemed to be following an unwritten code of its own that corresponded neither to the statute nor to good business practices.

But there was still much more information to be gathered

before we could move to making concrete recommendations. We needed to know more about the IOR's relation to other financial entities within the Roman curia, the layers of canon and civil law norms to which it was subject, its situation within the international legal and financial context, and whether it was or could be financially healthy enough to retain clients and be useful to the Holy See in the future. Over the next several weeks, a fuller picture came into view as we continued gathering information on financial performance, employee and management quality, account-holder behavior, and previous remediation efforts.

By February 2014, we had enough information to enable our three consultants—Clapis, Keeley, and Lena—to issue a detailed report in which they analyzed the legal, financial, and reputational risks to which the IOR was exposed. The report outlined four possible ways to proceed, with the pros and cons of each. Since there were several technical questions that had to be resolved before definitive recommendations could be made, the report concluded with a recommendation for immediate further studies on the avenues that seemed most advisable, including closure.

We sent the report to Pope Francis and his then eight-member council of cardinals from five continents, "the C-8," with a request to be authorized to proceed in accordance with our recommendation. The C-8, at their February meeting, instructed CRIOR to proceed with its plan to assemble a panel of experts to aid in determining the feasibility of the reform proposals we had identified as needing specific study. With that green light, we moved quickly to assemble a team of experts from a variety of specialized fields, including Italian and international tax law, Italian criminal law, banking law, canon law, financial regulation, and asset management. The readiness of well-qualified laypersons to assist pro bono in this project was impressive. Within a few weeks, our panel was ready to go.

The February meeting of the C-8 also yielded the most encouraging news about financial reforms to date: the creation of a Secretariat for the Economy, basically a centralized ministry of finance. It was to be headed by a take-charge Australian, Cardinal George Pell, who not only would have extensive powers but would be independent of the Secretariat of State (where some of us already suspected financial misconduct). Pell, a high-profile Catholic figure, with energy, intelligence, and a forceful personality, was just the person, I thought, to clean out the Holy See's Augean stables. And it was good to know that Pell, as a member of the pope's C-8, had voted to approve CRIOR's program for determining the future of the Vatican Bank.

Accordingly, CRIOR held the first meeting of its blue-ribbon panel. The venue was a large meeting room in the Casa Santa Marta. Pope Francis gave the group a good start, dropping in at the beginning to offer a few words of welcome and encouragement. The meeting itself was mainly devoted to getting acquainted and exchanging some preliminary ideas. As it wound up, it seemed that at last, after months of hard work, CRIOR was close to being able to offer specific, well-grounded recommendations to the pope regarding the closure or the reform of the IOR.

Meanwhile, however, Cardinal Pell and his advisers decided that there should be a single commission for all of the Vatican's financial and economic reforms, including those relating to the IOR. So, just two days after the meeting at Casa

Santa Marta, we were notified that CRIOR was to be disbanded. Pell then used the legal blueprint of our commission to create a new body that he called the Commission for Reference on the Organization of the Economic-Administrative Structure of the Holy See, or COSEA. At the same time, he established a small consultative body on the Way Forward for the IOR, nicknamed FIOR. It would be FIOR's job to make recommendations on the future of the Vatican Bank.

With hindsight, I can see that I may have made a mistake when I accepted Cardinal Pell's invitation to join FIOR. But I had met with him a number of times in Rome and Australia over the years, and I was impressed with his dedication to the Church, his independence of mind, and his can-do attitude. His plan to consolidate the reform process in one body seemed eminently reasonable to me. I was disappointed that he had closed CRIOR without looking at what we had learned and recommended, but I still thought he was the right person to move the financial reform process forward.

During the FIOR meetings in a small room near the top of the IOR tower, I came to think that Cardinal Pell was not receiving sound advice from his closest advisers. In fact, many of their proposals for the IOR were ideas our CRIOR group had examined and found wanting for reputational, legal, or financial reasons.

Presuming on my acquaintance with the cardinal, I tried my best to give him a fuller picture based on CRIOR's investigations. But I could not make headway against the men who had his ear day in and day out.

Though I did not realize it at the time, Cardinal Pell, despite his prominence in the Church, was, in a certain sense, a real outsider to the papal court. The rugged Australian, a former footballer, towered over most of his fellow prelates, and his blunt speech was as far from courtly circumlocution as Sydney from Rome. The same independence that suited him for the role of reformer aroused resentment among many courtiers, while his rather rough ways alienated others, making the work he wanted to accomplish all the more difficult.

For a time, it had looked as though Pell was going to be like Mark Twain's Connecticut Yankee, who was so clever that he ended up as prime minister in King Arthur's court. But as it turned out, Pell was more like the Americans in the novels of Henry James, who simply could not fathom the serpentine ways of characters formed in a culture very different from their own. In 2016, the pope would take away the extraordinary powers he had given Pell, and a year later the cardinal had to return to Australia to face charges of sexual abuse. Those charges ultimately did not stand up—but only after Pell had endured a trial ending in conviction, two appeals, and over a year in prison. In 2020, Australia's High Court reviewed the trial record, and unanimously found that a jury "acting rationally" would not have found enough evidence to convict him. Pell's conviction was quashed and an order of acquittal was entered.[3]

Looking back in 2021, Pell conceded, "I underestimated the ingenuity and resilience of the opponents of reform," adding that there had also been "opposition from people linked to corruption."[4]

Pell's chief antagonist in the reform process was the now-disgraced Cardinal Giovanni Becciu, who was holding the powerful position of *sostituto,* somewhat similar to the U.S. president's chief of staff. Becciu was stripped of the rights and privileges of a cardinal by Pope Francis in 2020, and as of this writing was on trial in the Vatican on charges of abuse of office, embezzlement, conspiracy, and witness tampering. He has steadfastly refused to explain the purpose of large sums of money (over $2 million) he authorized to be sent to an Australian security and intelligence firm at the time Pell was being investigated there. Becciu's insistence that the purpose of those payments is "classified" has led the Italian press to speculate that they were meant to influence the Pell investigation.[5]

Toward the end of June 2014, Cardinal Pell informed me that the IOR was to have an entirely new Board of Superintendence and that he wanted me to be a member. He said he felt obliged to let me know that he was putting me on the board over the strong objection of Jean-Baptiste de Franssu, a French money manager who had served on COSEA and who was now going to be the IOR's president. Because I had expressed disagreement with de Franssu on several points during the FIOR process, that news did not bode well. At that point, I believe that if Edward, with his great practical wisdom, had been alive to discuss the situation with me, I would have washed my hands of the IOR. But still coping with grief by working night and day, I accepted the invitation to serve.

On July 9, the Vatican officially announced the formation of the new IOR board and the appointment of its first members: de Franssu, British-Australian hedge fund billionaire Michael Hintze, the Deutsche Bank officer Clemens Boersig, and me. It was not a good sign that, on the very same day, there was an article in the *Süddeutsche Zeitung* on the likelihood that criminal charges would be brought against Boersig for having lied in court about Deutsche Bank's position in a much-publicized civil bankruptcy case.

To my mind, Deutsche Bank's scandal-ridden history alone would have suggested caution about Boersig's appointment.[6] The presumption of innocence to which he was entitled in a criminal proceeding was not relevant to the determination of whether his presence on the IOR board was advisable, especially since the Holy See was making great efforts to rehabilitate the IOR's reputation at the time.

My own quick internet search revealed other reasons for concern. The civil lawsuit against Boersig and others had ended in an enormous financial loss for Deutsche Bank. The heirs of German media baron Leo Kirch had charged the bank with intentionally maneuvering Kirch's company into bankruptcy, and had won a judgment in their favor, after which the bank had agreed to pay an out-of-court settlement of almost a billion euros.[7] My internet search also turned up an account of a speech by Boersig to women executives where—bad news for me—he discouraged them from seeking board positions!

Two months after his appointment to the IOR board, Boersig was indicted for the felonies of false testimony and conspiracy to provide false testimony in a civil proceeding.[8] After weeks passed without Boersig offering any explanation to the board, and to spare him the embarrassment of my making a request on the record, I sent him a polite email expressing my hope that he would provide the board with information on his legal situation. That was never done. When I approached de Franssu on the subject, he said he was satisfied with Boersig's personal assurance that the indictment would soon be dismissed. That did not happen.

Instead, Boersig became a defendant in a highly publicized criminal trial in Munich. The court proceedings, held in intermittent sessions, lasted from April 2015 to May 2016. In the end, some key witnesses failed to appear, and he was acquitted on the grounds that the evidence that had been sufficient for the large damage judgment against him in the civil suit did not meet the higher level of proof required for a criminal conviction.

During the many months when he was on trial, Boersig was the subject of much negative publicity in Germany, which—fortunately for the IOR—never found its way into the Italian press. The articles seldom failed to mention his position on the IOR board (e.g., "the most unpopular German banker . . . now on the Supervisory Board of the Vatican Bank where perhaps he will get an education in charity").[9] The German papers stressed that the loss of the civil suit plus the criminal prosecution (regardless of the eventual outcome of the latter) had severely damaged Deutsche Bank's already checkered reputation and that the extraordinary expenses of the settlement and the litigation had impaired the bank's financial position.

It was my view that, given the delicate situation of the IOR, the reputational risk of Boersig's presence on the board was great, and that it would have been the right thing to do for him to resign. Instead, he sat at the board's table for two years, except for times when he missed meetings in order to attend his trial. Perhaps someone in the IOR had a sense of humor, or perhaps it was just chance that there was a large painting of Christ crucified between two thieves on the wall behind Boersig's customary seat. He finally stepped down from the board a month after his acquittal.

Needless to say, my having raised questions about the matter did not endear me to the banker who already thought that women should not sit on boards. Thus, from the outset of my service, I was in the black books of Boersig and the president. My hopes rose somewhat when two more board members were appointed: Mauricio Larrain, a courtly banker from Chile with a master's degree from Harvard Law School; and Italian banker Carlo Salvatori, whose expertise on the Italian context was important for our work. Still, it was evident that I was never going to be a member of the club.

I sometimes raised my eyes to the frescoed ceiling of the boardroom, where a figure personifying the papacy as protector of the Church was surrounded by images representing faith, hope, and charity, and wondered how I would find the strength to persevere. It was especially discouraging that other members of the board seemed to be willing to overlook the IOR's governing statute whenever it got in the way of something they wished to do. Some were keen to "reform" the statute by eliminating its checks and balances.

Of my years on the IOR board, I can say little more, due to the fiduciary and confidentiality obligations of a director. For

Pope Francis opening the IOR board meeting with a prayer

much of that time, I was engaged in updating the IOR's basically sound governing statute, attempting to preserve its best features while bringing it into conformity with best international practices. In that endeavor, I would like to hope that I did some good. It was a promising sign when Moneyval reported after its 2021 inspection that the IOR had made good progress in eliminating the risks that are within Moneyval's purview, namely money laundering and terrorist financing.[10] But questions about the bank's financial health and quality of service remained. With IOR's profits down and customer assets dropping, the *Wall Street Journal*'s Vatican reporter pointed out, "Now it must convince legitimate customers, inside the Vatican and out, that it has something to offer them."[11]

When the board created committees, I became chair of the human resources and remuneration committee, which gave me some satisfaction, since I had gained a good sense of the concerns of the employees during the CRIOR investigation.

In that capacity, I had to deal with a situation that troubled me greatly. In November 2017, I was shocked to learn that Giulio Mattietti, the deputy director of the Vatican Bank, had been summarily dismissed by the general director, Gianfranco Mammi, without following normal termination procedures.

Mattietti was one of the IOR's most capable, respected, and well-liked employees. One of his longtime co-workers described him as the "most intelligent, reasonable and nicest man working not just in the IOR, but in the Vatican." Within the institute, the sudden and unexplained dismissal of Mattietti was widely believed to be caused by professional jealousy on the part of the insecure and unpopular Mammi.

Many in the IOR had been astonished when Pope Francis promoted Mammi, an undistinguished midlevel employee, to the directorship of the institute, passing over more experienced and credentialed candidates. But it was noted that Mammi was the man who had handled Cardinal Bergoglio's Argentinian financial affairs at the IOR and that the two had remained close. Mammi had ready access to the pope, and when Mattietti was fired without any reason given, it was widely believed that Mammi had secured the pope's personal approval for the dismissal.

Pope Francis himself seems to have been aware of Mammi's limitations, because he had taken the unusual step of appointing an adjunct to assist him. But the adjunct arrangement was increasingly uncomfortable for Mammi because the employees generally preferred to deal with Mattietti.

That the staff held Mammi in rather low esteem was evident from a fake letter that was circulating among them at the time. Perfectly mimicking Mammi's manner of speech, the letter purported to be a confession from him to the pope, asking pardon for various personal and professional misdeeds, concluding with "and Holy Father I confess that I can't even speak Italian very well." It must have been infuriating for Mammi to see the employees dropping into the adjunct's office day after day while he sat alone in his.

Mattietti's abrupt dismissal, coming on the heels of the much-publicized forced resignation of the Vatican's reformist auditor general, Libero Milone, became a big story, and led to wild speculation in the press about possible misconduct by Mattietti. In an effort to save his name and reputation, Mattietti immediately wrote Vatican authorities and went public to demand the grounds for his unexplained firing.[12]

Since the IOR board was responsible for overseeing IOR management, and since IOR regulations for termination of employees had not been followed, the board was obliged to look into the matter. As chair of the relevant committee, I prepared to gather the facts about what had happened. To my amazement, however, Pope Francis himself stepped in and ordered an immediate end to any investigation of the Mattietti case.

I must admit that there were occasions when I approved of Pope Francis's readiness to exercise his power as an absolute monarch, as when he chose the Mammi-Mattietti combination over outside candidates for the directorship. But this was a bitter pill indeed. Mattietti had been a courageous whistleblower in the time of Cipriani and Tulli, and he had worked hard to improve the IOR over the years. Now his reputation appeared irreparably harmed and his career prospects possibly ruined without any reason being given. Moreover, Mattietti's dismissal effectively consolidated power in Mammi, just as it had been under Cipriani.

What happened to Libero Milone and Giulio Mattietti sent a clear signal to the Vatican bureaucracy: if this could happen to such respected and intelligent employees without explanation, it could happen to anybody.

On February 7, 2018, I resigned from the IOR board. With my work on the legal framework of the IOR complete, I wrote, I believed that it was time to turn my attention to other matters. In my heart, I hoped that Mauricio Larrain, together with new board member Scott Malpass and other laypersons committed to the good of the Church, would eventually address the concerns that Clapis, Lena, Keeley, and I had identified and find a way to transform the troubled bank into a true Institute of Religious Works.

Later that year, there was a glimmer of hope. The Vatican withdrew all charges against Libero Milone, who had stoutly maintained that his treatment in 2017 was an attempt to block his investigations into Vatican finances, which reportedly were uncovering evidence of high-level corruption. Milone's alleged "crime" was attempting to violate "the private lives of officials of the Holy See" in the course of his investigations. One of those officials was Milone's chief accuser, Cardinal Becciu, who later testified that the order to fire Milone had come directly from the pope—the only person authorized to do so under Vatican law.[13] I only pray that one day the cloud will be lifted from Giulio Mattietti as it has been from Milone.

My time participating in the financial reform process in the Vatican taught me that the Holy See has long been trying to do too much with inadequate human resources in that area. Given that few prelates have an education that prepares them to deal with the finances of a sovereign state, the Holy See has always needed the assistance of lay experts. (I shudder when I recall that travel reimbursements in the early days of the PASS were handed to us in plain white envelopes containing U.S. dollars.)

But relying on outside financial experts brings its own difficulties. For one thing, most prelates are no more equipped to oversee financial experts than they are to handle complex financial matters themselves—as witness the history of the Vatican Bank, where laymen, in fact, turned out to be foxes in the chicken coop. And attempts to remedy the situation by bringing in expensive financial consulting firms ran into problems as well because most outside consultants were unfamiliar with the ecclesiastical system of governance (so differ-

ent from that of the business world) to which Holy See
financial entities are subject.

When Pope Pius XII founded the IOR in the midst of
World War II, there was good reason for the Holy See to
have a financial institution to handle its own funds and mon-
eys entrusted to it by various dioceses, congregations, religious orders, and parishes. Quite apart from wartime
instability, it was very difficult to arrange international trans-
fers of funds until the development of sophisticated payment
technology in the 1970s.

Under today's circumstances, however, the questions that
our Commission for Reference on the IOR was about to investigate before its closure in 2014 remain pertinent: How
does the IOR's performance in customer care and investment
compare with alternatives available to its clients? Does the
IOR perform any financial services that cannot now be safely,
reliably, and better performed by reputable financial institutions outside the Vatican?

Regarding the future of Vatican finances, much will depend on information gradually emerging in the long-running
Vatican trial of several defendants, including Cardinal Becciu, on charges of embezzlement, money laundering, abuse of
office, misappropriation, and fraud. That trial, ongoing at the
time of this writing, is expected to last for another year or
more. Meanwhile in 2022, in a singular expression of confidence in the management of the Vatican Bank (or lack of
confidence in the Secretariat of State), Pope Francis ordered
all Holy See institutions, including the Secretariat of State, to
transfer all their financial assets to the bank, whose client base
and net profits have declined in recent years.[14] In 2023, the

pope approved revisions to the IOR's statutes, reinforcing its relative independence from other Vatican departments.[15] The pope's confidence received a boost a few months later when the IOR's annual report showed a 63 percent increase in profits over the previous year.[16]

CHAPTER TWELVE

The Pope Addresses "Diseases of the Curia"

✤

*The Curia is called constantly to improve and to grow in
communion, holiness and wisdom, in order to carry out fully
its mission. And yet, like any body, like any human body, it is
also exposed to diseases.*

—POPE FRANCIS,
Christmas greetings to the Roman curia, 2014

On December 22, 2014, the members and staff of the curia
gathered to hear the papal Christmas greetings in the Sala
Clementina. They must have been looking forward to the
traditional message of thanks and encouragement along with
the usual papal Christmas gifts—a bottle of Asti Spumante
and a panettone studded with raisins and candied fruit. But
instead of a pontifical pat on the back, they got a stern lecture
on fifteen "diseases of the Curia."[17]

One can imagine the rising discomfort in the audience
while Pope Francis delivered his verbal lumps of coal. As he
described weakness after weakness, each listener must have
wondered what was coming next. Yet, at the end, they must
have felt that they had been let off pretty lightly. Here is the
pope's list (omitting his elaborations on the characteristics of
each disease):

1. "The disease of thinking we are 'immortal,' 'immune,' or
   downright 'indispensable.'"

2. "Another disease is the 'Martha complex,' excessive busyness."

3. "Then too there is the disease of mental and spiritual 'petrification.'"

4. "The disease of excessive planning and of functionalism."

5. "The disease of poor coordination."

6. "There is also a 'spiritual Alzheimer's disease.'"

7. "The disease of rivalry and vainglory."

8. "The disease of existential schizophrenia."

9. "The disease of gossiping, grumbling, and backbiting."

10. "The disease of idolizing superiors."

11. "The disease of indifference to others."

12. "The disease of a lugubrious face."

13. "The disease of hoarding."

14. "The disease of closed circles, where belonging to a clique becomes more powerful than belonging to the Body and, in some circumstances, to Christ himself."

15. "Lastly: the disease of worldly profit, of forms of self-exhibition."

Headlines around the world described the speech as a "blistering," "scathing" rebuke. It was said to be Pope Francis's "harshest criticism to date of the Vatican bureaucracy."[18]

Yet this was no fire-breathing sermon. There was no mention of two elephants in the room—financial misconduct and homosexuality in the priesthood, about which the pope had occasionally expressed concern.[19] As for the "seven deadly sins," a few were touched upon indirectly—as when he called "existential schizophrenia" a "most serious disease that often strikes those who abandon pastoral service and restrict themselves to bureaucratic matters, thus losing contact with reality, with concrete people. In this way they create their own parallel world, where they set aside all that they teach with severity to others and begin to live a hidden and often dissolute life." There was no suggestion that the defects on the pope's list, taken as a whole, amounted to an unhealthy *culture*. Savonarola would have given it a C-minus.

Some of the behaviors the pope criticized had already been modified, for courtiers in all ages can morph in a millisecond when they sense a new wind blowing through the palace corridors. Plutarch tells us that when Plato briefly became the favorite adviser of the Syracusan tyrant Dionysius, "modesty and temperance" began to be observed in feasts and banquets; "every man in the court was desirous to give himself to learning and philosophy"; and the royal palace was "full of sand and dust with the number of those who drew plats and figures of geometry."[20] Pope Francis's choice to live in Casa Santa Marta with its plain food, terrible coffee, and self-serve breakfasts and suppers, along with his simplicity of dress, sent powerful signals without a word ever spoken. Ecclesiastical finery was out; small cars were in.

The Christmas talk to the curia exemplifies why it is difficult for an outsider like me to form a clear picture of this enigmatic pope. Unlike Popes John Paul II and Benedict XVI, who taught, wrote, and spoke with great clarity and consistency, Pope Francis speaks more elliptically; his messages are often ambiguous or hard to interpret; his personality is more multifaceted; and he often seems to contradict himself. Although he has been a vigorous champion of human rights in some contexts, he has made unprecedented concessions to China while remaining silent about that country's treatment of its Uyghur population and other minorities. Just as it took many decades and much careful research for a fuller understanding of Pope Pius XII to emerge, it will likely be some time before enough is known to make a full appraisal of Pope Francis.

Regarding the curia, however, my experiences with the Institute of Religious Works, the Pontifical Academy of Social Sciences, and various committees and councils lead me to offer a few observations. While much good work has been done by and within Vatican departments over the years, a bureaucracy that was left to itself for more than three decades cannot help but develop pathologies. As the old saying goes: when the cat's away the mice will play. Some areas became little fiefdoms, and in some cases, as George Weigel has pointed out, councils within the Vatican have even created confusion about who speaks for the Church:

> The dynamics of modern bureaucracy took over such that, by the turn of the millennium, many of the pontifical councils were functioning like international non-governmental organizations, hosting numerous conferences and releasing streams of documents, while their presidents, who were usually cardinals, were becoming alternative or parallel spokesmen for "the Vatican" on a range of issues.[21]

Over the years, the effects of "the dynamics of modern bureaucracy" were compounded not only by the tendency of Popes John Paul II and Benedict XVI to repose excessive confidence in the heads of departments, but by the fact that the curia is not an ordinary bureaucracy. Thus, a first step toward reform of the curia would be to recognize it for what it is: the

court of an absolute monarch. Though the curia's "diseases"
in many respects resemble the ills that afflict other large organizations, many are the unique maladies of a court culture.[22]
A mistake made by many well-intentioned outside consultants has been to approach the Holy See as though it were a
business corporation, an NGO, or a municipality. But it will
take more than a handbook on good business practices, or a
visit from a McKinsey team, to bring the clerical culture of
the curia into conformity with the standards to which all of
its members are pledged as Catholic Christians.

One place to start would be to address the working conditions of the four thousand or so employees in Vatican City,
about half of whom are laymen and laywomen. After what I
observed as chair of the IOR's human resources committee, I
was not surprised in 2021 when John Allen, editor of the
Catholic news service *Crux,* called attention to "a largely un-
diagnosed human resources pandemic in the Vatican."[23]

Allen's article began with the story of American Monsignor Robert Oliver, who, after seven years of dedicated service in a demanding job on the Pontifical Commission for the
Protection of Minors, had to learn from newspaper reports
that he had not been reappointed to that body. It was not just
the shabby treatment of the monsignor that prompted Allen
to write. (Oliver himself, accustomed to the ways of the Vatican, shrugged it off and went on to a new position as a professor at St. John's Seminary in Boston.) It was the fact that such
treatment is routine in an institution committed to respecting
the dignity of workers. Allen said:

> If you think the biggest administrative problem facing
> the Vatican is ideological division or internal corrup-

tion, you've been reading too many potboilers. Sure, there are occasionally spectacular cases of fraud, deception, personal immorality, and so on, but the chief day-to-day problem—one so hard-wired into the system that, after a while, people don't even notice it—is that too often, rank-and-file personnel aren't treated as human beings, worthy of working conditions in which they can flourish and reach their potential, but as disposable cogs in a bureaucratic machine.

One relatively simple way to begin changing curial culture—or at least to improve the lives of a few thousand men and women—would be to assure rank-and-file personnel of "working conditions in which they can flourish and reach their potential." That would be a major step toward bringing the Vatican's own practices into conformity with what the Church has consistently proclaimed about the dignity of labor in its long tradition of Catholic social teaching. It would also send an important message to Church administrators at all levels. It would, however, require dealing with a problem that was mentioned neither by Allen nor by Pope Francis in his 2014 Christmas message: demeaning attitudes and behavior toward the women religious and laywomen employees who constitute about a quarter of the Vatican workforce.

The long-standing problems in that area came briefly into the spotlight in 2019 when the editor of a monthly supplement to the Vatican's official newspaper abruptly resigned with her entire female staff. *L'Osservatore Romano* had never had a female reporter until 2012, when Lucetta Scaraffia was hired in response to Pope Benedict's request "to give women more space in the paper."[24] Scaraffia was a perfect choice. A professor of history at Rome's La Sapienza University, she was a well-known public intellectual, a feminist, and a practicing Catholic. She embarked on the new job with enthusiasm. As she wrote seven years later, in a letter to Pope Francis explaining her resignation, she had been proud that the supplement she founded, *Donne Chiesa Mondo,* marked an important step for the Holy See: "For the first time, a group of women, who organized themselves autonomously and voted internally for filling positions and hiring new writers, was able to work in the heart of the Vatican and the Holy See's communications program. With free intelligence and heart."

But after a change in *L'Osservatore Romano*'s management in 2019, Scaraffia and her staff had come to feel "surrounded by a climate of mistrust and continual de-legitimization," especially after they published an article on sexual abuse of nuns by priests. "Under the new direction," she told the pope, "it seems to us that a vital initiative has been reduced to silence."

Scaraffia's very public resignation was of particular note because she was considered a rather conservative Catholic. I first met her in 2006, when we both spoke on feminism in the Church at one of the public forums sponsored by Rome's Centro di Orientamento Politico. On that occasion, she drew on her knowledge of history to present a fascinating overview of the Church's contributions to improving the status of women through the centuries. In a 2018 *New Yorker* interview, she described herself as a Catholic feminist who accepted the Church's teachings on such matters as the male priesthood, but who was "trying to fight patriarchy from the inside."[25]

A 2021 article by American attorney Jane Adolphe is a testimony to the problem's continued existence. Adolphe was an insider among insiders, as a consultant to, and later an employee of, the Holy See Secretariat of State from 2003 until her resignation in 2020. Her essay for the magazine *Inside the Vatican* began by welcoming Pope Francis's recent appointments of women to positions in the curia. But after praising this sign of progress, she went on to describe entrenched patterns of disrespectful behavior toward women that she had observed, concluding with her hope that the new appointments "might over time promote a more humane, professional, and respectful working environment," and that "these women whom Francis is hiring are eventually given the protections they need to carry out their duties, and the respect due for their professional competence and the God-given dignity they possess."[26]

Experiences like those of Lucetta Scaraffia and Jane Adolphe indicate that the curia still has a long way to go before living up to John Paul II's vision of complementarity between clergy and laity, and between men and women. Over a quarter century has passed since his 1995 exhortation to "all men in the Church to undergo, where necessary, a change of heart and to implement as a demand of their faith, a positive vision of women,"[27] and his even more explicit message in 1996 asking all departments of the Church to welcome the contributions of women: "It is urgently necessary to take certain concrete steps, beginning by providing room for women to participate in different fields and at all levels, including decision-making processes."[28]

Pope Francis, who had announced upon his election in 2013 that curial reform would be among his top priorities, partially delivered on that promise in 2022 with the issuance of a new constitution on the Roman curia. This document made several changes in the organization and structure of the curia, reducing the number of departments and redefining their scope. A key purpose of the constitution, according to the pope, is "in the spirit of a 'sound decentralization,' to leave to the competence of bishops the authority to resolve, in the exercise of 'their proper task as teachers' and pastors, those issues with which they are familiar."[29]

What attracted the most public attention, however, was the constitution's stress on the need for "the involvement of laywomen and laymen, even in roles of government and responsibility." Specifically, it provides that some departments "given their particular competence, power of governance and function" can be led by "any member of the faithful."

It will, however, take more than a new set of rules to change a deep-seated culture. Whether this new constitution—the product of nine years of work by the pope's Council of Advisers—will alleviate "diseases of the Curia," advance the "hour of the laity," or improve the circumstances of lay employees will depend on the character and competence of those who will be charged with its implementation. After the last reform of the Roman curia, in 1967, Pope Paul VI remarked, "It does no good to change faces if we don't change hearts." Where deference to local bishops in the spirit of subsidiarity is concerned, Vatican journalist John Allen in 2023 listed several instances where the pope's exercise of absolute authority apparently conflicted with his stated aim to respect the judgment of bishops in areas where they have competence.[30]

In light of numerous gaps between word and deed, Catholic women are sometimes asked how they can remain in a church where women "are treated like second-class citizens."

Flannery O'Connor, when confronted with that question, attacked its premise in her characteristically incisive way. She wrote to her friend, "Don't say the Church drags around this dead weight, just the Rev. So&So drags it around, or many Rev. So&Sos. The Church would as soon canonize a woman as a man and I suppose has done more than any other force in history to free women."[31]

O'Connor was referring to such things as the Church's success in gaining acceptance for the ideal of monogamy and for the belief that marriage is indissoluble—an astonishing achievement in the ancient world, where polygamy was common and men were permitted to put aside their wives. Later, in its rules governing separation from bed and board, the Church introduced standards of fidelity and decent treatment that were unknown to the secular law. At the Council of Trent, the Church defied heavy pressure from powerful princes and merchants to insist that a valid marriage requires the consent of both spouses.

The best answer, however, belongs to the Apostle Peter:

> Many of his disciples broke away and would not remain in his company any longer. Jesus then said to the Twelve, "Do you want to leave me too?" Simon Peter answered him, "Lord, to whom shall we go? You have the words of eternal life." (John 6:66–68)

There will always be "Rev. So&Sos" in the Catholic Church, just as there are So&Sos of both sexes in any organization. That is why the Church "is always in need of being purified, and incessantly pursues the path of penance and renewal."[32] But Catholics do not worship a church or its ministers. We worship the loving God, who sent his only begotten Son into the world "not to condemn the world, but that the world might be saved through him" (John 3:17).

The Church that is always in need of renewal is, of course, not just the institution, but the *ecclesia,* the entire people called together. Church leaders have often referred to Vatican II as initiating the "hour of the laity," but what would such an hour look like?

The Hour of the Laity

✤

We'd look pretty foolish without them.

—SAINT JOHN HENRY NEWMAN
in response to the bishop who asked what he thought of the laity[1]

*Who is going to save the Church? Not our bishops, not our
priests and religious! It is up to you, the lay people! You have
the minds, the eyes, the ears to save the Church!*

—VENERABLE BISHOP FULTON SHEEN,
Address to Knights of Columbus, 1972

The main objective of the Second Vatican Council was to better prepare the Church for the evangelization of the modern world, and the laity were expected to be in the forefront of that effort. As one of its youngest members, the future Pope John Paul II, declared, "With the Council, *the hour of the laity* truly struck."[2]

Today, it often seems that the clock stopped somewhere along the way, at least in Western countries. In Europe and North America, increasing numbers of men and women identify themselves as nonreligious or unaffiliated with organized religion. In 2021, when one of the few still-living council fathers was asked to name the greatest challenge facing the Church today, his reply sounded as though not much had changed since the council ended in 1965. Nigerian Cardinal Francis Arinze said: "Convince each member of the Church to do his or her own specific part in the general mission of the Church, that is, lay faithful (who are 99% of the Church), clerics and religious. And convince the clergy of the importance of the lay apostolate."[3]

In a sense, Cardinal Arinze was only stating the obvious. The challenge is the same today as it was at the beginning of Christianity—to spread the message of the gospel. What has changed, dramatically, is the environment in which the mission must be carried out.

Early in the nineteenth century, John Henry Newman, the British theologian for whom the Newman centers at many colleges are named, strove in vain to convince Church leaders to get ready for a time of increasing skepticism and disbelief. First as an Anglican minister, and later as a Catholic priest, he warned that while Christianity had surmounted grave perils in the past, it had never yet experienced what was then emerging in Europe: "a world simply irreligious."[4] Paganism, after all, had been open to transcendence: "It was full of superstition, not infidelity." The coming era would be very different.

Newman's hope for the future lay in the fact that time and again it had been the lay faithful and their parish priests who held fast to the faith and handed it on in troubled periods.[5] So he devoted much of his writing to the need to prepare the faithful to be a transformative presence in the modern world. What was needed, he said, was "a laity who know their religion, who enter into it, who know just where they stand, who know what they hold, and what they do not, who know their creed so well that they can give an account of it, who know so much of history that they can defend it."[6] Above all, they should "cherish a vivid sense of God above, and keep in mind that you have souls to be judged and to be saved."

Vatican II was woefully late in addressing the situation that Newman and others had forecast. While the council fathers were striving to come to terms with the challenge of a world falling into unbelief, a cultural revolution was already gathering force. No sooner did the council close its doors in 1965 than Church leaders were confronting a tsunami of challenges to moral and religious ideas about sex, marriage, honor, and personal responsibility. That was the situation facing each of the three popes discussed in this book.

By 1978, when Karol Wojtyla was elected pope, the cultural revolution was in full swing. John Paul II immediately made the need for a new evangelization a central theme of his pontificate. In his first encyclical, he proposed treating the years leading up to the two thousandth anniversary of the birth of Christ as a "new Advent."[7] As the jubilee approached, he repeatedly called the faithful to a "springtime of evangelization," by which he said he meant a "renewed commitment *to apply,* as faithfully as possible, *the teachings of Vatican II to the life of every individual and of the whole Church.*"[8] The process of preparing for the new millennium, he said, had "really begun in the Second Vatican Council," and had "*become as it were a hermeneutical key of my Pontificate*" (emphases in original).

Like Newman, John Paul II recognized that the laity would need to be better prepared if they were to be in the forefront of the new evangelization. He promoted the teachings of Vatican II in ways that made those documents fresh for late-twentieth-century listeners. He raised the profile of the Pontifical Council for the Laity and appointed a layman to be its chief administrator. He initiated the immensely popular World Youth Days, inspiring countless young men and women around the world to a deeper engagement with their faith. Within the Vatican, he appointed a number of lay men and women to positions that had previously been held by clergy, and he established a practice of meeting regularly in Castel Gandolfo and around his own dinner table to exchange views with lay experts of all faiths and in all fields of human activity. He broke new ground by appointing women to positions that had previously been held by men (such as my appointments to head the Vatican delegation to the UN's Conference on Women in Beijing and to the presidency of the Pontifical Academy of Social Sciences).

His example caught on with many bishops, and it inspired two generations of younger priests. By respecting both the laity's primary responsibility for renewal of the secular sphere and the unique role of the priest as a minister of the sacraments, he laid the groundwork for further complementarity between clergy and laity, and men and women, at all levels of the Church.

Those innovations came naturally to the Polish pope, not only because of his involvement in Vatican II, but even more because of his own personal history of lifelong friendship and collaboration with laymen and laywomen.

When Joseph Ratzinger was elected Pope Benedict XVI in 2005 at age seventy-eight (the oldest since 1730), he had already made substantial contributions to the religious formation of the laity through his scholarship, addressing the challenges of the modern age, the relationship between faith and reason, and the danger of what he called the "dictatorship of relativism." During his eight-year pontificate, his writings and speeches showed a remarkable ability to communicate with all kinds of audiences at all levels of education. Building on the work of his predecessor, he established a Pontifical Council for the Promotion of the New Evangelization to assist the laity in countries undergoing "a progressive secularization of society and a sort of eclipse of the sense of God." (In 2022, under Pope Francis's new Constitution for the Curia, that council was merged into a new Dicastery for Evangelization.)

As we have seen, the burdens of office, and the need to deal with the clerical sex abuse crisis and emerging financial scandals, absorbed much of Pope Benedict's time and energy. Eventually, those responsibilities weighed on him so heavily that he resigned the papacy in 2013.

Looking back over the efforts of Popes John Paul II and Benedict XVI to promote the aims of the council in which they had participated participated (Wojtyla as a young bishop and Ratzinger as a very young theological adviser), it seems to me that each made impressive strides in finding ways to express the truths of the Catholic faith in terms that could engage modern men and women. Each, in his writings and public witness, spoke with a clear, consistent voice, both on matters of doctrine and on the issues of the day. Both were distinguished scholars who left behind a rich body of philosophical and theological writing. Both pontificates saw significant advances in ecumenism and in Christian-Jewish relations. And both popes welcomed what Pope Benedict called the "good gifts of the Enlightenment," a marriage of faith and reason that enabled them to build on those elements of modernity that were conducive to human dignity and flourishing while countering the elements that were destructive of those ends. But as recounted earlier, their extensive delegation of administrative responsibilities had some unfortunate consequences.

In terms of the traditional image of the Church as *Mater et*

Magistra, mother and teacher, one might say that when Pope Benedict resigned in 2013, the Vatican was well supplied with doctrinal guidance but in dire need of someone who would take charge of the household.

That year, when Argentinian Cardinal Jorge Bergoglio became Pope Francis, he made it clear from the beginning that reform of the papal court would be high on his agenda. Early in his pontificate, he established a commission to prepare a new Constitution of the Roman Curia, and after nine years of work, that document was promulgated in 2022. There were no surprises. For, as the accompanying announcement stated, the constitution had "already been almost entirely implemented over the past nine years, through the mergers and adjustments that have taken place and have led to the creation of new dicasteries."[9]

The constitution's title, *Praedicate Evangelium,* "Preach the Gospel," together with the announcement that the central idea of the reform was to make the Church suitable for the evangelization of today's secularized world, suggested a desire for continuity with the teachings of Vatican II. The document itself does not reveal how reorganization of the Vatican bureaucracy was expected to advance evangelization, but it is reasonable to suppose that will depend, as under the previous constitution, on the competence and character of the persons named to fill the new, or renamed, posts.

In that connection, the part of the constitution that attracted the most comment was its expansion of opportunities for laypersons to hold roles in the curia, including the possibility of heading certain departments. As is apparent from the foregoing chapters, Holy See officials, whose training has done little to prepare them for administering a sovereign state in the twenty-first century, could certainly benefit from expert lay assistance in many areas. One might even imagine that increased complementarity with laypersons would help to improve morale within the curia. For no one who has spent much time within the walls of Vatican City can fail to observe what Emeritus Pope Benedict noted in a recent interview—that the Church's "bureaucracy is spent and tired."[10] On the other hand, the history of Vatican reliance on laymen in the area of finance suggests caution about how expanded lay participation in government will work out in practice.

Compared to his predecessors, Pope Francis has given relatively little attention to setting conditions for the preparation of a laity that is equipped and inspired to be protagonists of evangelization. As noted earlier, his statements on matters of faith and morals have often been ambiguous or contradictory. His decision to abolish the Council for the Laity and to fold its responsibilities into a new Dicastery for the Laity, the Family and Life was understandable as an economic measure, but it inevitably gave the impression of downgrading the importance of the bodies it replaced. It was not as though the reasons the fathers of Vatican II had urged the creation of a "special secretariat" for the laity were no longer urgent.

That last point brings me to the need to offer a few words of encouragement for the students and friends whose questions about service to the Church prompted me to write this account of my involvement with the Holy See. Over the years I've had countless conversations with young Catholic women and men concerned about the challenges facing their Church and eager to devote some of their time and talents to Church service. For the most part, these young people were not contemplating religious vocations or Church employment;

rather, they were looking forward to marriage, family life, and what they hoped would be meaningful work in secular settings. They all said they sensed that this is a time when the Church's need for lay assistance is especially great.

And they were right. For one thing, laypeople, with their varied skills and talents, can enable the clergy to do more of what they are called to do, what they have been trained to do, and what they know how to do best.

That came home to me one evening when my husband and I were sitting in the kitchen of our newly purchased house and heard a knock at the back door. It was an elderly priest who had stopped by to visit the former owners, not realizing that they had moved. We invited him in for a cup of tea and learned that he was the chief financial officer of a nearby college. My Jewish husband, who admired priests and religious sisters for their sacrifices, was curious. He asked the man how being the CFO of a college fit with the way he had imagined the priesthood when he was young. The old man looked a bit rueful and said, "Well, the way it happened was the college needed someone for the job and they knew my family owned a business in Brookline." Perhaps that worked out well for all concerned, but Edward's question about the man's vocation went to the heart of the matter.

For the layperson contemplating service to the Church at any level, the first question he or she must face is how that would fit within the context of one's baptismal calling to holiness and mission. That is a matter for each person's discernment—depending on one's capabilities, opportunities, inclinations, and personal and occupational responsibilities, and not least on where one is on one's journey through life. The kinds of services I felt able to offer, and the time I had available, were very different when I was raising children from what they had been when I was a young, single lawyer, and from what they were when my children were older and on their own. I was in my fifties before I began the work for my local church that led to my involvement with the Holy See.

The fact that this reflection on my service to the Holy See includes setbacks as well as advances, disappointments as well as satisfactions, should not be discouraging to anyone who is drawn to offer his or her services where they may be needed. When setting out on a journey, it's important to have a sense of the terrain ahead and to prepare accordingly. And the experiences of other travelers can often be helpful in that process.

Where disappointments are concerned, it's important to be aware that disappointment in service for the Church can easily shade into disillusion or cynicism. On that point we have the testimony of an insightful Catholic writer who spent over forty-one years working full-time for the Church and Church-related organizations. Over that time, Francis X. Maier saw both the best and the worst of ecclesiastical life. He recently offered these wise words for anyone who might be considering a path similar to his:

> The layperson who serves around or within the structures of the Church needs a vivid daily prayer life to sustain a sense of zeal and mission. When these flag in the persons who inhabit or collaborate with her structures, the ability of the Church to be a leaven in the culture very quickly declines. When you don't pray, you become a cynic; you focus on material results to the exclusion of God's role in the success or failure of your work. Eccle-

sial bureaucracies, I suspect, can have a *higher*—not a lower—percentage of practical atheists among their number than the general Catholic population, for exactly this reason. Which is why every lay Church worker, adviser, and volunteer also needs to cultivate humility, patience, and a sense of humor.[11]

Maier's remark about the extent of practical atheism in ecclesial bureaucracies may be startling to some. But I imagine that is what Pope Francis was really getting at in his message on "diseases of the Curia" when he spoke of "spiritual Alzheimer's." Pope Paul VI had put it more bluntly long ago, noting that "the loss of the faith is spreading throughout the world and into the highest levels within the Church."[12]

Maier also cautions that anyone hoping to solve long-standing problems quickly will be disappointed: "The chronic, underlying illness of the Church in our country, in our day, isn't prone to quick fixes, and real lay 'power' doesn't reside in money or professional skill or positions of influence within or over a Church bureaucracy. It proceeds from a personal witness of holiness."[13]

For the same reason, I would add that a layperson contemplating service to the Church must also cultivate patience and perseverance. In that connection, I have found it helpful to bear in mind the thoughts of Jesuit philosopher Bernard Lonergan on the challenges of living amid the intellectual turmoil and breakdown of certainties that attend any period of cultural crisis:

There is bound to be formed a solid right that is determined to live in a world that no longer exists. There is bound to be formed a scattered left, captivated by now this, now that new development, exploring now this and now that new possibility. But what will count is a perhaps not numerous center, big enough to be at home in both the old and the new, painstaking enough to work out one by one the transitions to be made.[14]

Where lay service for the Holy See in particular is concerned, I cannot disagree with veteran Vaticanista John Allen's observation that "you could make a pretty good case that your odds of accomplishing something positive in the Catholic Church actually increase by a percentage point for every 25 miles or so of distance you put between yourself and Rome."[15]

It's also important to avoid an exaggerated idea of what one can accomplish. No one has said it better than Pope Saint John Paul II: "There is a temptation which perennially besets every spiritual journey and pastoral work: that of thinking that the results depend on our ability to act and to plan. God of course asks us really to cooperate with his grace, and therefore invites us to invest all our resources of intelligence and energy in serving the cause of the Kingdom. But it is fatal to forget that 'without Christ we can do nothing.' "[16]

Finally, it should be said that no one should shy away from service to the Church at any level out of a sense that things are so bad that their efforts would be wasted. One has only to read the Acts of the Apostles or Alessandro Manzoni's great Italian novel *The Betrothed* to be reminded that a few ordinary people willing to live in truth and to call good and evil by name can help to shift probabilities in a better direction.

Notes

Part I: The Court of John Paul II

1. Letter to Mary Ann Glendon and the Holy See Delegation to the Fourth World Conference on Women, in *John Paul II and the Genius of Women* (Washington, D.C.: U.S. Conference of Catholic Bishops, 1997), 62.
2. George Weigel, *The End and the Beginning* (New York: Doubleday, 2010), 530, n. 10.
3. Mary Ann Glendon, "Contrition in the Age of Spin Control," *First Things,* November 1997, 10.
4. John Paul II, Address to the Pontifical Academy of Social Sciences, November 25, 1994, in Proceedings of the First Plenary Session of the Pontifical Academy of Social Sciences (Libreria Editrice Vaticana, 1996), 33.
5. Mary Ann Glendon, "The Right to Work and the Limits of Law," in *Work and Human Fulfillment,* Edmond Malinvaud and Margaret Archer, eds. (Sapientia Press, 2003), 145.
6. Edmond Malinvaud, Report by the President, in Proceedings of the Second Plenary Session of the Pontifical Academy of Social Sciences (Libreria Editrice Vaticana, 1997), 44–45.
7. Edmond Malinvaud, Report by the President, in Proceedings of the Fourth Plenary Session of the Pontifical Academy of Social Sciences (Libreria Editrice Vaticana, 1999), 32.
8. *Work and Human Fulfillment,* Edmond Malinvaud and Margaret Archer, eds. (Sapientia Press, 2003), 5.
9. Edmond Malinvaud, Report by the President, in *Democracy: Reality and Responsibility,* Proceedings of the Sixth Plenary Session of the Pontifical Academy of Social Sciences (Libreria Editrice Vaticana, 2001), xxx–xxxiii.
10. Hans F. Zacher, Preface to *Democracy: Reality and Responsibility,* xii.

11. Edmond Malinvaud, Report by the President, in Proceedings of the Seventh Plenary Session of the Pontifical Academy of Social Sciences (Libreria Editrice Vaticana, 2002), 33.

12. As recounted by Edmond Malinvaud, ibid., 31.

13. Mary Ann Glendon, Final Report, in Pontifical Academy of Social Sciences, *Intergenerational Solidarity, Welfare and Human Ecology,* Mary Ann Glendon, ed. (Libreria Editrice Vaticana, 2004), 354–69.

14. U.S. President's Council on Bioethics, *Taking Care: Ethical Caregiving in Our Aging Society* (Washington, D.C.: 2005), 5.

Part II: The Court of Benedict XVI

1. The story has been well told by former Ambassador James Nicholson in *The United States and the Holy See: The Long Road,* 2nd ed. (Rome: Trenta Giorni, 2004); and Massimo Franco, *Parallel Empires: The Vatican and the United States—Two Centuries of Alliance and Conflict* (New York: Doubleday, 2008).

2. Nicholson, *United States and the Holy See,* 13.

3. Lettera di Abraham Lincoln a Pontefice Pio IX, November 16, 1863, located in the Archivo Segreto Vaticano, Epistolae ad Principes, Positiones et Minutae 50, n. 124 (copy supplied to the author by Massimo Franco).

4. Joseph P. Lash, *Eleanor: The Years Alone* (New York: Konecky & Konecky, 1972), 278.

5. Eleanor Roosevelt to Harry Truman, January 29, 1952, National Archives Catalog, https://catalog.archives.gov/id/4708721.

6. Quoted in Nicholson, *United States and the Holy See,* 56.

7. Ibid., 59.

8. *Americans United for the Separation of Church and State et al. v. Ronald Reagan et al.,* 786 F. 2d 194 (3rd Cir. 1986).

9. Colin Powell, Preface to Nicholson, *United States and the Holy See,* 7.

10. J. C. Hooker to William H. Seward, September 1, 1865, in United States Ministers to the Papal States Stock, American Catholic Historical Association Documents, vol. 1, p. 346.

11. Address of His Holiness Benedict XVI to H.E. Mrs. Mary Ann Glendon, New Ambassador of the United States of America to the Holy See, *L'Osservatore Romano,* March 1, 2008, 2.

12. Ibid.

13. Address of Ambassador Mary Ann Glendon to His Holiness Benedict XVI, *L'Osservatore Romano,* March 1, 2008, 2.

14. Elizabeth Lev, "The Vatican Through an Ambassador's Eye," Zenit News Agency, March 6, 2009.

15. "Largest Donors of Humanitarian Aid Worldwide in 2022 (in million U.S. dollars), by country," *Statista,* January 5, 2023, https://www.statista.com/statistics/275597/largers-donor-countries-of-aid-world wide.

16. As accurately predicted by Delia Gallagher in "A Teaching Pope," *Inside the Vatican,* April 2008, 13.

17. Benedict XVI, Message to the People of the United States, April 8, 2008.

18. Benedict XVI, Interview with Journalists, April 15, 2008.

19. Benedict XVI, Address on South Lawn of White House, April 16, 2008.

20. Ibid., and cf. *Spe Salvi,* 24.

21. Benedict XVI, Address to the United States Bishops, April 16, 2008.

22. Benedict XVI, Address to the General Assembly of the United Nations, April 18, 2008.

23. Benedict XVI, Homily at Saint Patrick's Cathedral, April 19, 2008.

24. The gendarmerie are the police force of the Vatican City State, not to be confused with the Swiss Guards, who act as the pope's personal bodyguards and the security service for the Holy See.

25. Massimo Franco, "Bush dal Pontefice: una visita familiare," *Corriere della Sera,* June 14, 2008, 1.

26. Orazio la Rocca, Visita dal Papa, Disagio in Vaticano: "Accoglienza troppo calorosa" *La Repubblica,* June 12, 2008, 10.

27. George W. Bush, Remarks at National Catholic Prayer Breakfast, May 28, 2005, https://www.govinfo.gov/content/pkg/PPP-2005-book1/html/PPP-2005-book1-doc-pg835-2.htm.

28. Francis X. Rocca, "For Bush and Benedict, a Personal and Political Bond," Religion News Service, June 5, 2008.

29. Winston Lord, Interview with Center for Public Diplomacy, June 4, 2019, https://uscpublicdiplomacy.org/story/qa-cpd-winston-lord.

30. *Pope Benedict XVI's Legal Thought,* Marta Cartabia and Andrea Simoncini, eds. (Cambridge, U.K.: Cambridge University Press, 2015).

31. Pope Benedict XVI, Address to the General Assembly of the United Nations, April 18, 2008.

32. Václav Havel, Words on Words, Speech of October 25 1989, translated and published in *The New York Review of Books*, January 18, 1990.

33. For details, see Mary Ann Glendon, "The Forgotten Crucible: The

Latin American Influence on the Universal Human Rights Idea," *Harvard Human Rights Journal,* vol. 16 (2003): 27–39.

34. Center for Applied Research in the Apostolate, Frequently Requested Church Statistics, http://cara.georgetown.edu/frequently-requested -church-statistics.

35. *Deus Caritas Est,* 28 (b).

36. Mary Ann Glendon, *A World Made New: Eleanor Roosevelt and the Universal Declaration of Human Rights* (New York: Random House, 2001), chs. 10 and 12.

37. Pope Benedict XVI, Interview with Journalists, April 15, 2008.

38. Pope Benedict XVI, White House Address, April 16, 2008.

39. Pope Benedict XVI, General Audience, April 30, 2008.

40. Pope Benedict XVI, Address to the United States Bishops, April 16, 2008.

41. The following year in Milan, Cardinal Ruini gave a ringing defense of positive secularism in a public dialogue with secularist thinker Ernesto Galli della Loggia, published as *Confini: Dialogo sul cristian- esimo e il mondo contemporaneo* (Milan: Mondadori, 2009).

42. Joseph Augustine Di Noia, O.P., "Charity and Justice in the Relations Among Peoples and Nations," in Proceedings of the Thirteenth Ple- nary Session of the Pontifical Academy of Social Sciences (Libreria Editrice Vaticana, 2007), 12, 15–17.

43. George Weigel, *Witness to Hope* (New York: Harper Collins, 1999), 150, 234, 854–57.

44. Ibid., 855.

45. Quoted in John Byron Kuhner, Pope Benedict's Resignation Speech, *Inside the Vatican,* March–April 2022, 44.

Part III: The Court of Pope Francis

1. Quoted with other portions of the July 28, 2013, press conference in Robert Moynihan, "A 'Penned-in' Pope?" *Inside the Vatican,* March– April 2022, 3.

2. "Vatican Official Praises China for Witness to Catholic Social Teach- ing," Catholic News Agency, Feb 6, 2018, https://www.catholicnews agency.com/news/37694/vatican-official-praises-china-for-witness-to -catholic-social-teaching; Philip Pullella, "Unholy War of Words Breaks Out over Vatican Rapprochement with China," Reuters, Feb- ruary 8, 2018, https://www.reuters.com/article/us-pope-china/unholy

-war-of-words-breaks-out-over-vatican-rapprochement-with-china
-idUSKBN1FS2F4.

3. *Pell v. the Queen, High Court of Australia* [2020], 268 Commonwealth
Law Reports 123, 127.

4. Quoted in Elise Ann Allen, "Cardinal Pell Says He 'Underestimated'
Opponents to His Vatican Financial Reform Attempts," *Crux*, September 24, 2021, https://cruxnow.com/vatican/2021/09/cardinal-pell
-says-he-underestimated-opponents-to-his-vatican-financial-reform
-attempts.

5. Becciu's "'Classified' Tech Company Linked to Trump-Russia Alle-
gations," *The Pillar*, February 15, 2022.

6. An account of the controversies can be found on Wikipedia,
"Deutsche Bank," https://en.wikipedia.org/wiki/Deutsche_Bank.

7. Martin Hesse and Stefan Kaiser, "Deutsche Bank und Leo Kirch:
Jürgen Fitschen und Ackermann vor Gericht," *Der Spiegel*, April 28,
2015, https://www.spiegel.de/wirtschaft/kirch-und-deutsche-bank
-fitschen-und-ackermann-vor-gericht-a-1030484.html.

8. Christian Rickens, "Prozess Gegen Fitschen: Kirchs Langer Schat-
ten," *Der Spiegel*, April 28, 2015, http://www.spiegel.de/wirtschaft
/unternehmen/prozess-gegen-fitschen-kirchs-langer-schatten
-a-1030956.html.

9. "Deutsche Bank: Die Angeklagten im Neuen Kirch-Prozess,"
Wirtschaftswoche, April 28, 2015, http://www.wiwo.de/unternehmen
/banken/deutsche-bank-die-angeklagten-im-neuen-kirch-prozess
/11685288.html.

10. "EU Financial Watchdog Upgrades Vatican Status to 'Regular,'" *The
Pillar*, May 9, 2022, https://www.pillarcatholic.com/p/eu-financial
-watchdog-upgrades-vatican.

11. Francis X. Rocca, "Cleaned-Up Vatican Bank Works to Justify Its
Existence," *Wall Street Journal*, June 26, 2021 (emphasis in original),
https://www.wsj.com/articles/cleaned-up-vatican-bank-works-to
-justify-its-existence-11624699801.

12. "IOR, Mattietti Writes to the Board: I Don't Know Why They Fired
Me," *La Stampa*, December 13, 2017, https://www.lastampa.it
/vatican-insider/en/2017/12/13/news/ior-mattietti-writes-to-the
-board-i-don-t-know-why-they-fired-me-1.34082676.

13. "Becciu Blames Pope Francis, Staff, Bad Memory in Vatican Trial,"
The Pillar, May 19, 2022, https://www.pillarcatholic.com/p/becciu
-blames-pope-francis-staff.

14. Hannah Brockhaus, "Pope Francis Instructs Vatican Entities to Move All Funds to Vatican Bank by Sept. 30," Catholic News Agency, August 23, 2022, https://www.catholicnewsagency.com/news/252093/pope-francis-instructs-vatican-entities-to-move-all-funds-to-vatican-bank-by-sept-30.

15. Andrea Gagliarducci, "A New(ish) Statute for the Vatican Bank: Here's What It Means," Catholic News Agency, March 7, 2023, https://www.catholicnewsagency.com/news/253812/a-newish-statute-for-the-vatican-bank-here-s-what-it-means.

16. "Vatican Bank Reports Profits of Progress," *The Pillar,* June 7, 2023, https://www.pillarcatholic.com/p/vatican-bank-reports-profits-of-progress.

17. Pope Francis, Christmas Greetings to the Roman Curia, December 22, 2014, https://www.vatican.va/content/francesco/en/speeches/2014/december/documents/papa-francesco_20141222_curia-romana.html.

18. Deborah Ball and Tamara Audi, "Pope Issues Blistering Critique of Vatican Bureaucracy," *Wall Street Journal,* December 23, 2014, https://www.wsj.com/articles/pope-issues-blistering-critique-of-vatican-bureaucracy-1419278268.

19. Agence France-Presse, "Gay People Should Not Join Catholic Clergy, Pope Francis Says," *Guardian,* December 2, 2018, https://www.theguardian.com/world/2018/dec/02/gay-people-should-not-join-catholic-clergy-pope-francis-says.

20. "Life of Dionysius," in *Plutarch's Lives,* vol. 8 (New York: Limited Editions Club, 1941), 267, 303–5; and "Life of Dion," vol. 7, 240–41.

21. George Weigel, *God's Choice: Pope Benedict XVI and the Future of the Catholic Church* (New York: HarperCollins, 2005), 245.

22. Norbert Elias, *The Court Society* (New York: Pantheon, 1969). See also John Julius Norwich, *Absolute Monarchs: A History of the Papacy* (New York: Random House, 2011).

23. John L. Allen Jr., "Shabby Exit of Anti-Abuse Reformer Captures Vatican's HR Pandemic," *Crux,* April 8, 2021, https://cruxnow.com/news-analysis/2021/04/shabby-exit-of-anti-abuse-reformer-captures-vaticans-hr-pandemic. See also Loup Besmond de Senneville, "Winds of Revolt Blowing Among Vatican's Lay Employees," La Croix International, May 24, 2021, https://international.la-croix.com/news/religion/winds-of-revolt-blowing-among-vaticans-lay-employees/14360.

24. Thomas D. Williams, "Founder of Vatican Women's Magazine Quits

over Return to 'Male Control,'" Breitbart, March 27, 2019, https://
www.breitbart.com/faith/2019/03/27/founder-of-vatican-womens
-magazine-quits-over-return-to-male-control.

25. Elizabeth Barber, "Lucetta Scaraffia Is Trying to Fight Catholic Patriarchy from the Inside," *New Yorker,* October 28, 2018, https://www
.newyorker.com/culture/persons-of-interest/lucetta-scaraffia-is-trying
-to-fight-catholic-patriarchy-from-the-inside.

26. Jane Adolphe, "The Movement to Appoint More Women to Vatican
Posts: Who Benefits?," *Inside the Vatican,* May–June 2021, 16–20.

27. Letter to Mary Ann Glendon and the Holy See Delegation to the
Fourth World Conference on Women, in *John Paul II and the Genius
of Women* (Washington, D.C.: U.S. Conference of Catholic Bishops,
1997), 62.

28. *Vita Consecrata,* 58.

29. Ed. Condon, "Does Roche's Rescript Dispense with Vatican II?," *The
Pillar,* February 22, 2023, https://www.pillarcatholic.com/does-roches
-rescript-dispense-with-vatican-ii/?ref=the-pillar-post-newsletter.

30. John L. Allen Jr. "As Synodality Summit Looms, Navigating a Papacy's Imperial Phase," *Crux,* February 26, 2023, https://cruxnow
.com/news-analysis/2023/02/as-synodality-summit-looms-navigating
-a-papacys-imperial-phase.

31. Flannery O'Connor, *The Habit of Being* (New York: Farrar, Straus
and Giroux, 1979), 168.

32. *Lumen Gentium,* 13.

Epilogue: The Hour of the Laity

1. Recounted in John Coulson, Introduction to John Henry Newman,
On Consulting the Faithful in Matters of Doctrine (New York: Sheed
and Ward, 1961), 18–19.

2. John Paul II, Homily, Jubilee of the Apostolate of the Laity (2000).

3. Barbara Middleton, "Interview: Cardinal Francis Arinze, an 'Elder
Statesman' of the Church," *Inside the Vatican,* May–June 2021, 31.

4. John Henry Newman, "Sermon on the Opening of St. Bernard's Seminary," https://www.newmanreader.org/works/ninesermons/sermon9
.html.

5. John Henry Newman, *Arians of the Fourth Century* (Sydney: Went-
worth Press, 2019).

6. John Henry Newman, "Duties of Catholics Toward the Protestant
View," https://www.newmanreader.org/works/england/lecture9.html.

7. *Redemptor Hominis,* 1.

8. *Tertio Millennio Adveniente,* 23.

9. Andrea Tornielli and Sergio Centofanti, "Pope Francis Promulgates Apostolic Constitution on Roman Curia 'Praedicate Evangelium,'" *Vatican News,* March 19, 2022, https://www.vaticannews.va/en/pope /news/2022-03/pope-francis-promulgates-constitution-praedicate -evangelium.html.

10. Pope Benedict XVI, *Light of the World: The Pope, the Church, and the Signs of the Times: An Interview with Peter Seewald* (San Francisco: Ignatius Press, 2010), 5.

11. Francis X. Maier, "Thoughts on the Lay Vocation," The Catholic Thing, February 5, 2020, https://www.thecatholicthing.org/2020/02/05 /thoughts-on-the-lay-vocation.

12. Pope Paul VI, Address on the Sixtieth Anniversary of the Fatima Apparitions, October 13, 1977.

13. Francis X. Maier, "Thoughts on the Lay Vocation."

14. Bernard Lonergan, *Dimensions of Meaning in Collection: Papers of Bernard Lonergan, S. J.* (New York: Herder and Herder, 1967), 267.

15. John L. Allen Jr., "Shabby Exit of Anti-Abuse Reformer Captures Vatican's HR Pandemic," *Crux,* April 8, 2021, https://cruxnow.com /news-analysis/2021/04/shabby-exit-of-anti-abuse-reformer-captures -vaticans-hr-pandemic.

16. John Paul II, *Nuevo Millennio Ineunte,* 38.

Index

Note: page numbers in *italics* indicate photos.

ABOUT THE AUTHOR

MARY ANN GLENDON is Learned Hand Professor of Law emerita at Harvard University and a former U.S. Ambassador to the Holy See. In 1995, she led the Vatican delegation to Beijing for the UN's World Conference on Women, becoming the first woman ever to lead a Vatican delegation. Her books include *The Transformation of Family Law,* winner of the Order of the Coif Prize, the legal academy's highest award for scholarship; *Rights Talk; A Nation Under Lawyers; A World Made New: Eleanor Roosevelt and the Universal Declaration of Human Rights;* and *The Forum and the Tower,* a series of biographical essays exploring the relation between political philosophy and politics in action. She lives in Chestnut Hill, Massachusetts.